Channel I
OCCUPA
REVIEW
No.20

Published by the

CHANNEL ISLANDS OCCUPATION SOCIETY
(GUERNSEY)

Founded 1961

February 1995

CHANNEL ISLANDS OCCUPATION SOCIETY

1992 COMMITTEES

ISBN 0 9503948 5 8

Published by the Channel Islands Occupation Society (Guernsey) 1995

Typeset and printed by the Guernsey Press Company Limited,
Braye Road, Vale, Guernsey, C.I.

CONTENTS

Cover illustrations: **The German cartoon map on the front cover will shortly be published in full size facsimile (Scale 1:25000) – details from the Secretary of the Guernsey Branch.**
The back cover is the frontispiece to the *Festung Guernsey* section on the Mirus Battery; very much an artist's impression and inaccurate in detail.

The map on page 52 was drawn by Colin Partridge.

EDITORIAL

This issue of the *Occupation Review* breaks new ground with the use of inset full colour pages which enables us for the first time to publish some of the wealth of coloured material in *Festung Guernsey*, the official German handbook on their defences produced in 1944. At the time it served little purpose other than to provide the Islands' Commander-in-Chief with an exclusive coffee-table book to divert guests at his residence at La Corbinerie; now however the two surviving copies are an invaluable historical record and a detailed analysis of these volumes begins in this issue.

Fifty years after the deportations of September, 1942, an extensive diary kept by a Methodist minister from 1940 to 1945 was deposited at the Priaulx Library. Orginally earmarked for deportation, the Reverend Douglas Ord was ultimately exempted, and we publish extracts from his diary on those critical days. By contrast we also include the story of a local couple, Eric and Ruth Sirett, deported to Germany three months after their marriage; as they made their farewells they joked to friends that Hitler had invited them to the Continent for a delayed honeymoon! Although they made the best of it, none of the 900 or so deportees from Guernsey knew what fate awaited them as they were rounded up, just as a few months earlier three Jewish refugees had been removed to France to an equally unknown future. In the event the British were sent to relatively benign internment camps; the refugees went to Auschwitz.

1992 was the Year of the Archives, with the release of classified files in London – which as usual disappointed those expecting lurid revelations – and the release by the States of Guernsey of all administrative records from the Occupation years. Of these the files of the identity card system, which have survived almost complete, provide a unique record of the civilian population, including photographs of all adults. By way of introduction, a summary of the registration system appears in this issue. Unrestrained by any concept of data protection, the Germans used the registry to select candidates for deportation, including, somewhat ironically, Major Alick Stockwell who had presided over the creation of the identity card registry in 1940.

German notions of order and logic required that Island roads be systematically numbered and signposted, and in this issue the result in Jersey is described. Perhaps the Guernseyman's reluctance to number or even prominently signpost his roads is a reaction to the alien regimentation endured from 1940 to 1945.

Finally, we must apologise for the late appearance of this *Occupation Review*; we are grateful for your forbearance and can only hope that the result was worth waiting for.

K.T.

FESTUNG GUERNSEY 1944 – AN ANALYSIS OF THE OFFICIAL GERMAN HANDBOOK ON THEIR ISLAND FORTRESS – PART 1

Pierre Renier

Many people who have bought publications on the Occupation of these Islands will no doubt have seen references to this work among the credits. The reader may, therefore, already have an inkling as to the contents of the *Festung Guernsey* volumes. Only two copies are known to exist of this handbook, both held in Guernsey, and this article is intended to give an insight into the history and contents of *Festung Guernsey,* for the benefit both of those unfamiliar with the *Occupation Review* and those already interested in the Occupation.

By the late summer of 1944 the Allied armies had finally driven the Germans from Normandy. The German 84th Army Corps, of which the 319th Infantry Division in the Channel Islands had been a subordinate unit since May, 1942, had ceased to exist with the closing of the Falaise pocket in Normandy on 22nd August, 1944. By 25th August all four Allied armies in Normandy had drawn level with the River Seine, and Paris was liberated that day. More than a million men had taken part in the German defence of Normandy; of these 240,000 were dead or wounded and a further 200,000 were missing or captured. 25 of the 38 German divisions committed to the battle had been completely destroyed. By October most German units had been driven out of France, leaving only a few garrisons holding small but heavily fortified areas, designated as *Festungen* or fortresses, which were in effect being besieged by the Allies. Amongst this group of occupied areas were the Channel Islands, whose garrison escaped the heavy fighting experienced by their comrades on the French mainland at, for example, Brest and Le Havre. Indeed the 319th was nicknamed 'the Canada Division' because they were already effectively prisoners of war, cut off and surrounded by the Allies.

By August, 1944, Allied Intelligence had compiled from various sources a reasonably accurate map of the German defences of Guernsey. With this to hand it is plain why the Allied planners decided to leave the Islands alone. Ralph Palmer, in his memoir 'A Shopkeeper at Sea', pp.26-7, writes that, while serving as part of the planned Liberation Force based in Plymouth, "I became more and more impatient at the delay and could not understand why we did not come across and take over. Then one day, while reporting to the Naval barracks at Devonport for orders for an exercise, I saw a map of Guernsey . . . It showed known fortifications, gun sites and other concrete works of art with which the Island had been decorated – after that I waited patiently!"

ORIGINS OF FESTUNG GUERNSEY

Ironically, even as people were risking their lives to gather intelligence on the Island's defences, the Germans were themselves compiling what amounted to a guide book to their defences. About the time that Ralph Palmer saw the map of Guernsey's defences in 1944, Lieutenant-General Graf von Schmettow, Commanding Officer of the 319th Division and German Commander-in-Chief in the Channel Islands, had already set in hand the compilation of detailed accounts of the Islands' defences, known as *Festung Guernsey* and *Festung Jersey.*

This is confirmed by Baron von Aufsess in his book 'The von Aufsess Occupation Diary', p. 95, where he records on 15th December, 1944, calling upon von Schmettow while on a visit to Guernsey from his base in Jersey. "The General took me upstairs to his private study" (in the country house known as La Corbinerie) "and showed me a magnificent work which has been produced under his auspices: 'Fortress Jersey and Guernsey'. The best artists and photographers have been commissioned as contributors to this highly artistic multi-volume book."

For the Guernsey edition this was placed under the direction of Lieutenant-Colonel Hübner, senior staff officer (G.S.O.1) in von Schmettow's command. This was his rank in November, 1944; the *Einsatzgliederung* (Order of Battle Chart) of 1st September, 1944, his actual position and rank was 1a (Divisional Chief of Staff) Major Hübner. The team responsible was drawn from the *Divisionskartenstelle* (Divisional Cartographic Section) of the 319th Division. The personnel involved are listed in the detailed bookplate in *Festung Guernsey*, which names fourteen non-commissioned officers in the various disciplines of drawing, photography, printing and development, calligraphy and general craftwork.

The bookplate describes the work as "Fortress Guernsey – containing an account of the British Channel Island of Guernsey in words, drawings and photographs assembled in four volumes . . ."

GENERAL DESCRIPTION OF FESTUNG GUERNSEY

There are two known examples of Festung Guernsey. One is held at the Priaulx Library and is arranged in four volumes; the other is in the Royal Court Library and is sturdily bound in two large volumes. Both copies have the same layout, and indeed careful comparison shows that the text, which is typewritten, is identical, with that of the Royal Court

The Royal Court edition of Festung Guernsey, opened at the illustration of the two storey Divisionsgefechtsstand or divisional battle headquarters at La Corbinerie, St. Martin's. Now the headquarters of the Guernsey Civil Defence Organisation. This edition is bound in leather (from a car seat?) in two volumes within a sturdy slipcase.

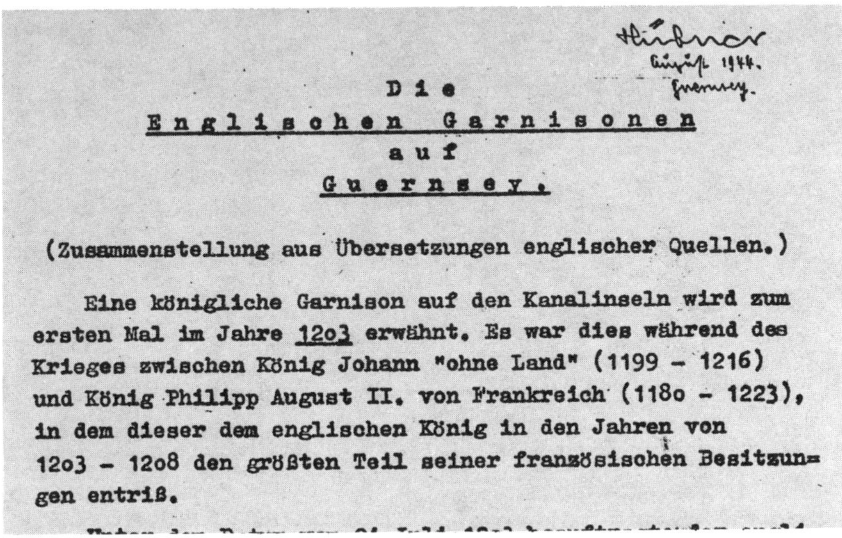

Hübner
August 1944.
Guernsey.

Die
Englischen Garnisonen
auf
Guernsey.

(Zusammenstellung aus Übersetzungen englischer Quellen.)

Eine königliche Garnison auf den Kanalinseln wird zum ersten Mal im Jahre 12o3 erwähnt. Es war dies während des Krieges zwischen König Johann "ohne Land" (1199 – 1216) und König Philipp August II. von Frankreich (118o – 1223), in dem dieser dem englischen König in den Jahren von 12o3 – 12o8 den größten Teil seiner französischen Besitzungen entriß.

First page of the essay on the English Garrisons of Guernsey, with the signature of Major Hübner and the date, August 1944, in the top right hand corner.

copy literally being a carbon copy of that at the Priaulx Library, with each and every typing error faithfully reproduced. The *Inhaltsverzeichnis*, or list of contents at the front of each of the four volumes or slipcases of the Priaulx Library copy can be assumed to represent the intended final layout; each section or *Heft* is paperbound and the sections are in turn grouped into four volumes or *Bände*; the sections are not bound in volumes in the Priaulx Library copy, instead each volume is represented by a slipcase.

In terms of content the text of both copies is essentially similar. However, the pictorial content differs in important respects. This is fortunate for the historian, because comparison of the two copies gives different perspectives of the same subject. When maps are compared, discrepancies suggest that units were on the move when the maps were being compiled; these differences help in tracing military dispositions over time. Each volume contains many original photographic prints; here again comparison reveals that although broadly the same subjects are depicted, the prints in each copy are not from the same negative but appear to be different images from the same roll of film. The end result is that the two existing copies of *Festung Guernsey* each cover the same topics, but are sufficiently dissimilar each to form a unique record.

CASTLE CORNET VON ST. PETER PORT GESEHEN

Reproduction of English print of circa 1740.

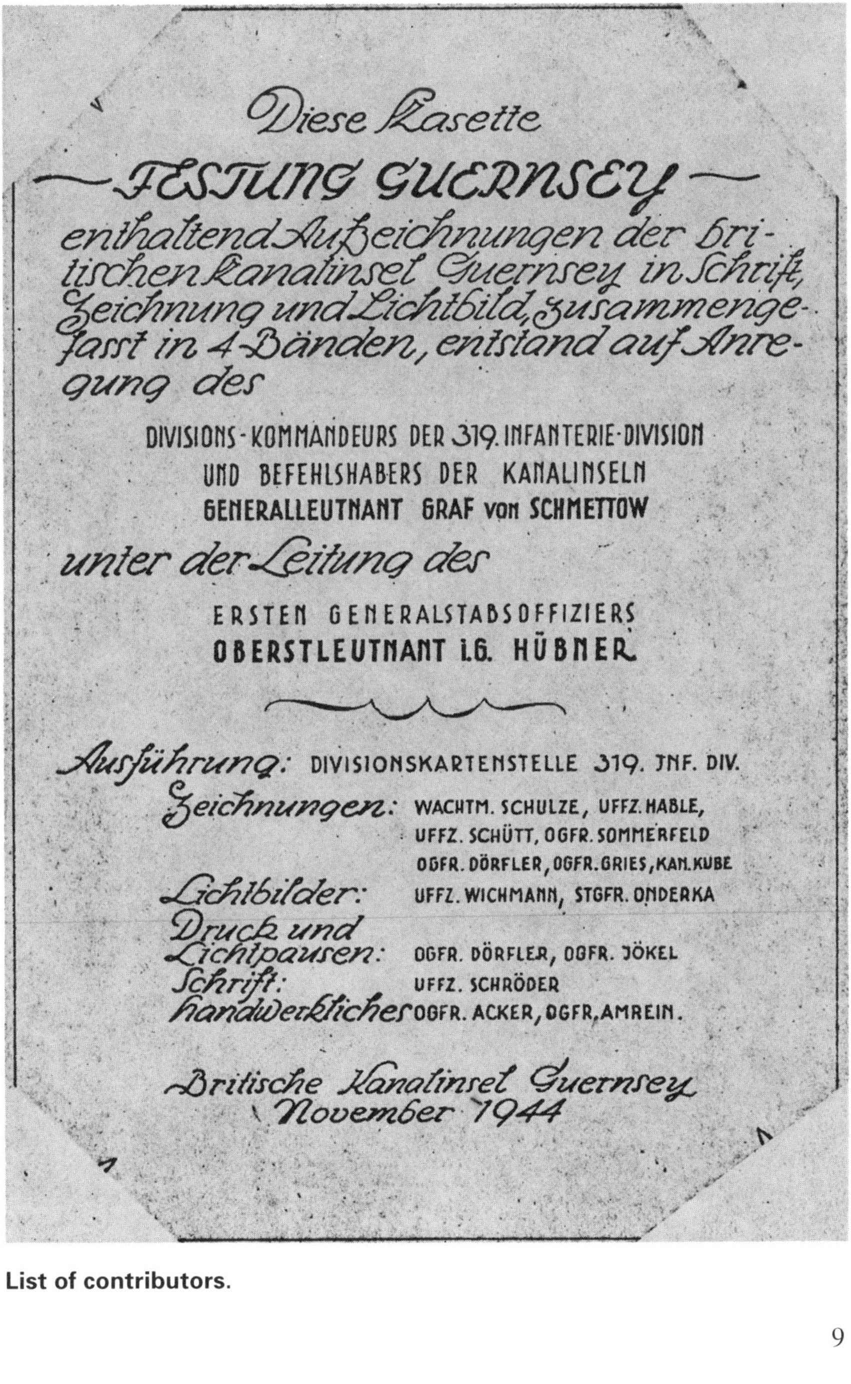

Diese Kasette

— FESTUNG GUERNSEY —

enthaltend Aufzeichnungen der britischen Kanalinsel Guernsey in Schrift, Zeichnung und Lichtbild, zusammengefasst in 4 Bänden, entstand auf Anregung des

DIVISIONS-KOMMANDEURS DER 319. INFANTERIE-DIVISION
UND BEFEHLSHABERS DER KANALINSELN
GENERALLEUTNANT GRAF VON SCHMETTOW

unter der Leitung des

ERSTEN GENERALSTABSOFFIZIERS
OBERSTLEUTNANT I.G. HÜBNER

Ausführung: DIVISIONSKARTENSTELLE 319. INF. DIV.
Zeichnungen: WACHTM. SCHULZE, UFFZ. HABLE, UFFZ. SCHÜTT, OGFR. SOMMERFELD OGFR. DÖRFLER, OGFR. GRIES, KAN. KUBE
Lichtbilder: UFFZ. WICHMANN, STGFR. ONDERKA
Druck und Lichtpausen: OGFR. DÖRFLER, OGFR. JÖKEL
Schrift: UFFZ. SCHRÖDER
handwerkliches OGFR. ACKER, OGFR. AMREIN.

Britische Kanalinsel Guernsey
November 1944

List of contributors.

CONTENTS OF FESTUNG GUERNSEY

The following abbreviations are used in the table below, listing the contents of *Festung Guernsey*:-

PL = Priaulx Library edition
RC = Royal Court Library edition
y = Details present in volumes held
n = Details not present in volumes held
Sect. = Section for reference use only, i.e. 3.3.6. = Band III Heft 3 Page 6

Volume	Part	Subject Title	Sect.	PL	RC
Band I	Heft 1	Die Englischen Garnisonen auf Guernsey	1.1	y	y
	Heft 2	Allgemeines über die Insel Guernsey	1.2	n	y
	Heft 3	Taktische Übersichten der Festungsbereiche	1.3	y	y
	Heft 4	Festungsmäßige Bauten	1.4	n	y
Band II	Heft 1	Eingesetzte Waffen	2.1	n	y
	Heft 2	Batterie Mirus	2.2	y	y
	Heft 3	Einsatz der Artillerie	2.3	n	y
	Heft 4	Einsatz der Flak-Artillerie	2.4	n	y
Band III	Heft 1	Hafen St. Peter Port von Terres Point bis Peterseck	3.1	y	y
	Heft 2	Schönbucht von Gemäuer bis Krevelberg	3.2	y	y
	Heft 3	St Sampsons Bordeaux-Hafen von Krevelberg bis Nebelhorn	3.3	n	y
	Heft 4	Ankerbucht von Nebelhorn bis Golfwerk	3.4	y	y
	Heft 5	Großbucht von Krähennest bis Houmet	3.5	y	y
	Heft 6	Vale-Abschnitt von Houmet bis Großfels	3.6	n	y
Band IV	Heft 1	Cobo-und Rundbucht von Großfels bis Reichenberg	4.1	y	y
	Heft 2	Perlebucht von Reichenberg bis Langenberg	4.2	n	y
	Heft 3	Felsenbucht von Langenberg bis Kaiserhof	4.3	n	y
	Heft 4	Westberg von Batterie Dollmann bis Schützenhof	4.4	n	y
	Heft 5	Torteval von Schützenhof bis Rabenstein	4.5	n	y
	Heft 6	Südbucht von Südkap bis Icart	4.6	n	y
	Heft 7	Mühlenbucht von Icart bis Straßburg	4.7	n	y
	Heft 8	Fermenbucht von Straßburg bis Fort George	4.8	y	y

The first volume of *Festung Guernsey* covers the history of the garrisons of Guernsey from the 13th Century up to the D-Day landings on 6th June, 1944. This is coupled with a tactical appraisal of the Islands' contribution to the Atlantic Wall and details of just some of the fortification work undertaken up to the time the work was compiled. The second volume looks at the military hardware, from flare pistols to the 30.5cm guns of *Batterie Mirus* and from flamethrowers to searchlights. The last two volumes examine in turn each *Stützpunkt*

		feldmäß.	festungsmäß. Schartenstde. fertig	im Bau	gepl. -30.A.	Zusammen	
10,5 cm K 331 f	ALDERNEY	3	13	–	–	16	davon = 1 auf Rü[…]
	GUERNSEY / Sark	13 / 2	21	–	–	34 / 2	" 1 " " / " 2 " "
	JERSEY	12	18	–	–	30	" 4 " "
		30	52	–	–	82	" 8 " "
4,7 cm Pak t	ALDERNEY	6	3	–	–	9	
	GUERNSEY	17	16	–	–	33	
	JERSEY	8	15	–	–	23	
		31	34	–	–	65	
5 cm Pak 38	ALDERNEY	4	1	–	–	5	
	GUERNSEY	15	–	–	–	15	
	JERSEY	10	–	–	–	10	
		29	1	–	–	30	
7,5 cm Pak 40	ALDERNEY	–	2	–	–	2	
	GUERNSEY	8	–	–	–	8	
	JERSEY	9	3	–	–	12	
		17	5	–	–	22	
Beton (in cbm rde. Zahl)	ALDERNEY	28 000	58 000			86 000	
	GUERNSEY	47 000	225 000			272 000	
	JERSEY	43 000	212 000			255 000	
		118 000	495 000			613 000	

Stand: 1. 9. 44

Table of artillery pieces emplaced on each island, distinguishing between those in mobile or field positions, and those in fortress standard emplacements. The initials "f" and "t" denote captured French and Czechoslovak weapons respectively. (Priaulx Library).

(strongpoint) and *Widerstandsnest* (resistance point) around the Island's coastline, anti-clockwise from St. Peter Port. Each coastal section details the units involved, together with their strength, location, weaponry and battle instructions as at 1st September, 1944. These coastal volumes contain such a copious supply of information that they will be looked at in detail in a second article on *Festung Guernsey* to be published in a subsequent edition of the *Occupation Review*.

DETAILED PAGE BY PAGE ANALYSIS OF FESTUNG GUERNSEY

The following abbreviations are used in the page by page analysis:-

PLp = Priaulx Library copy page number
RCp = Royal Court Library copy page number
ctd = continued
ni = not included in this copy
TP = Title page
1.3.7 = Volume 1 section 3 page 7
1.1.12R = Volume 1 section 1 reverse of page 12) } Example of page references

SECTION 1.1

Die Englischen Garnisonen auf Guernsey (The English Garrisons on Guernsey)

PLP	RCp	Description of contents	
TP	15	Colour print of St Peter Port from Castle Cornet entitled 'Die Englischen Garnisonen auf Guernsey'.	
1/24	16/36	Essay on the garrisoning of Guernsey from the 13th to 19th centuries, compiled from translations of English sources.	
25	37	Map of the Island of Guernsey showing the fortifications from Berry's History of Guernsey, 1814.	
26	38	Übersicht der alten Befestigungen: (Survey of the old fortifications), Guernsey,	map at 1:50000 scale
27	51	Mont Crevelt	map at 1:2500 scale
28	50	Vale Castle	map at 1:2500 scale
29	49	Fort Doyle	map at 1:2500 scale
30	48	Fort Le Marchant	map at 1:2500 scale
31	ni	Fort Pembroke	map at 1:2500 scale
ni	47	Nid de l'Herbe Battery	map at 1:2500 scale
32	45	Star Fort	map at 1:2500 scale
ni	46	Grande Rocque Battery	map at 1:2500 scale
33	44	Fort Hommet	map at 1:2500 scale
34	43	Fort Le Crocq	map at 1:2500 scale
35	43ctd	Fort Richmond	map at 1:2500 scale
36	42	Perelle Battery	map at 1:2500 scale

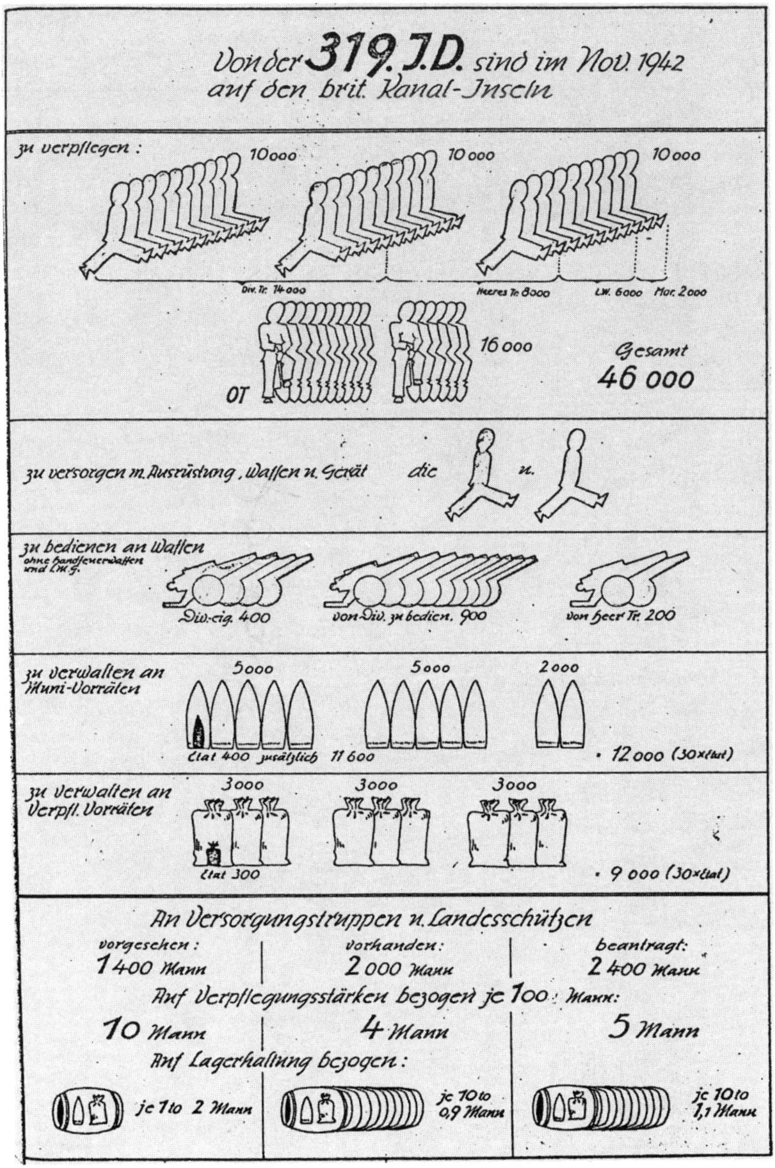

The logistical task. A diagram illustrating the men and weapons of the garrison in November 1942 and their supply requirements. The total strength was 46,000, including 15,000 workers of the Organisation Todt. (Priaulx Library).

PLp	RCp	Description of contents	
36ctd	ni	Brock Battery	map at 1:2500 scale
37	41	Fort Saumarez	map at 1:2500 scale
38	52	Castle Cornet	map at 1:2500 scale
39	40	Fort Grey	map at 1:2500 scale
ni	39	Fort Pézeries	map at 1:2500 scale
ni	54	Jerbourg Battery	map at 1:2500 scale
40	53	Fort George	map at 1:2500 scale

The essay on the English garrisons includes details of Island militias and summarises the military history of Guernsey, including successive French invasions after the English Crown had lost many of its territories in France.

The writer also quotes at length from the standing orders of the Royalist garrison of Castle Cornet in 1643 at the beginning of the eight year siege of the castle by the Parliamentarians of Guernsey, which threatened severe punishment for lapses in discipline, including amputation of the right hand and even execution. This may perhaps have been of more than academic interest to the German garrison in 1944 as they prepared to face an Allied invasion. The essay is illustrated by reproductions of historic maps, views of Castle Cornet in the 18th century and of St Sampson's Church, and drawings depicting uniforms of the Royal Guernsey Militia.

SECTION 1.2

Allgemeines über die Insel Guernsey (General information on the Island of Guernsey)

PLp	RCp	Description of contents
m	1	Colour map of Guernsey, postcard size, showing the island parishes.
i		
s	2	Photographs qty. 2 (in RC).
s	3/5	Übersetzung aus einem englischen Konversationslexikon
i		über die Kanalinseln (Translated from an English
n		Encyclopedia on the Channel Islands). Essay on general
g		aspects of the islands.
	5/6	Geologie (Subsection on the islands' geology)
	6	Klima (Subsection on the islands' climate)
h	6/7	Flora und Fauna (Subsection on the islands' plants and animals)
e	7/10	Regierung (Subsection on the islands' government)
f	10	Sprache (Subsection on the islands' language)
t	10/14	Geschichte (Subsection on the islands' history)

A relatively small section, much of which appears to be directly translated from the article on the Channel Islands in the Encyclopedia

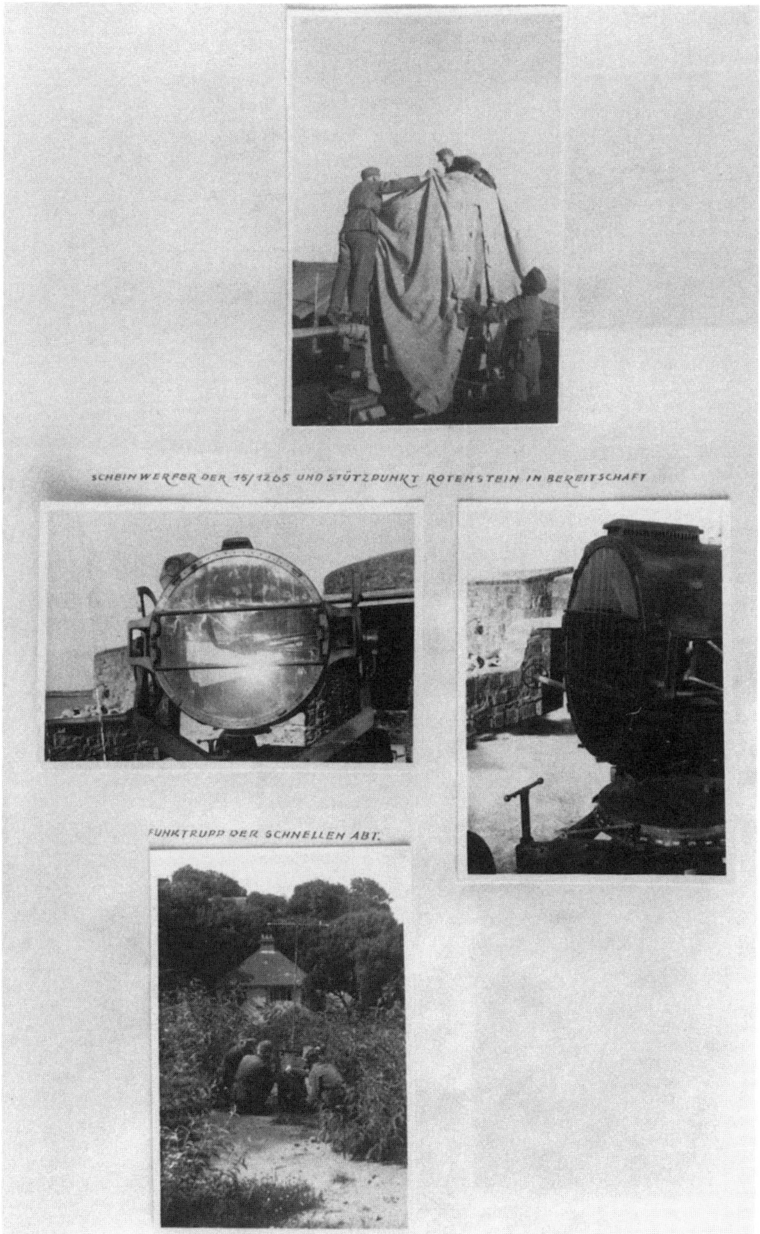

Searchlight at Fort Hommet. Typical page of original prints.

Britannica 13th edition (London and New York, 1926). Again as in section 1.1. the aim is to continue with the broader aspects of the island's history and geography, setting the picture for the following sections.

One point raised by this section is the last page of the RC edition, where the narrative stops in mid-flow. This is not the only occasion when this occurs and may indicate that this edition was compiled in haste.

SECTION 1.3

Taktische Übersichten der Festungsbereiche (Tactical summary of the fortress area)

PLp	RCp	Description of contents
TP	100	Colour map of the Bay of St Malo, postcard size, showing the Channel Islands and adjacent coast of France.
1/2	101	Allgemein-geographische und taktische Angaben über die Festungen Guernsey, Jersey und Alderney – Stand 1.9.44. (General geographical and tactical information on the fortresses of Guernsey, Jersey and Alderney as at 1.9.44.)
		A. Geographisches: 1. Lage: (Position of islands in relation to France and England at 1:2500000 scale.)
		2. Grösse: (Size, table showing area in sq. km. of islands and length of coastline.)
3	102	3. Küstengestaltung: (Coastal features, gives details of the large sandy bays together with how many units could land at the same time, height of the islands relative to each other and size of population.)
		4. Nautische und Wetterverhältnisse: (Nautical and weather conditions, details of tidal ranges and losses of men due to very changeable weather.)
3/4	102/103	5. Historisches: (Historical details up to time of invasion on 6.6.1944, such as details of air raids and resultant casualties, main individuals killed and vessels lost, sea engagements, losses to sea mines, enemy raids and vessels beached.)
4	103	B. Besatzungen (Garrison):
		1. Aufklärung: (Tactical reconnaissance, gives details of number of radar and searchlight units in each island.)
		2. Sicherung: (Security, harbour defence boats only located near the harbour)
		3. Artillerie: (Artillery, details of number of batteries in each island used for heavy area fire, heavy high-angle fire and light artillery.)

PLp	RCp	Description of contents
5	104	4. Landeabwehrgeschütze: (Coastal defence guns, details of light artillery pieces and ground position weaponry for infantry.)
		5. Infanterie: (Infantry, details of unit sizes in each island.)
		6. Reserven: (Reserves, details of infantry reserves, tank units, rapid movement units and anti-tank strengths.)
5/6	104/105	7. Flak: (Anti-aircraft defences, details of quantities of A.A. employed in the islands' density of A.A. per sq. km., civil protection and air raid protection for the troops.)
6	105	8. Mineneinsatz: (Mine dispositions, details of total number laid in each island.)
		9. Gesamtbesatzung: (Total garrison details, giving number of army, airforce, naval and construction personnel in the island.)
7	106	Guernsey, map at 1:50000 scale (Showing areas covered under section 1.3.1./3 (part A.1./3: Lage, Größe, Küstengestaltgung.)
8	ni	Einsatzgliederung Guernsey stand 1.9.44: (Order of battle for units in Guernsey as at 1.9.44.)
9	111	Artillerie-einsatz Guernsey, map at 1:50000 scale: (Operational artillery, map showing where each unit is deployed.)
10	112	Flak-einsatz Guernsey, map at 1:50000 scale: (Operational A.A., map showing where each unit is deployed.)
ni	110	Infanterie-einsatz Guernsey, map at 1:50000 scale: (Operational infantry map showing where each unit is deployed.)
11	108	Ansichten von Guernsey nach einer englischen seekarte: (Views of Guernsey taken from an English chart showing northern aspects of the island.)
12	107	As 1.3.11, but aspects of Guernsey from south-west and east.
13	113	Jersey, map at 1:50000 scale: (Details as for 1.3.7.)
14	ni	Infanterie-einsatz Jersey, map at 1:50000 scale.
15	ni	Artillerie-einsatz Jersey, map at 1:50000 scale.
16	ni	Flak-einsatz Jersey, map at 1:50000 scale.
17	ni	Leuchtfeuer im Bereich der Kanalinseln, map at 1:50000 scale. (Light beacons in the area of the Channel Islands.)
18	ni	Wirkungsbereiche d.H.K., Mar.Art.u.Flak, map at 1:500000 scale: (Map showing the effective range of the Heeres Küsten (Army Coastal) Marine (Naval) Artillerie and Flak units weaponry varying from 16km for 88mm flak pieces to 42km (extreme range) for the 305mm guns of Batterie Mirus.)

Festungsmäßige Bauten – artist's impression of a building site on the title page of the section dealing with permanent fortifications.

Extract from fortification map showing south-east coast of Guernsey. The circles marking each site are coded red for the Army, green for the Air Force (generally flak batteries) and blue for the Navy (coastal artillery battery at Jerbourg). The details listed for each site are coded red for fortress standard structures and green for field standard structures.

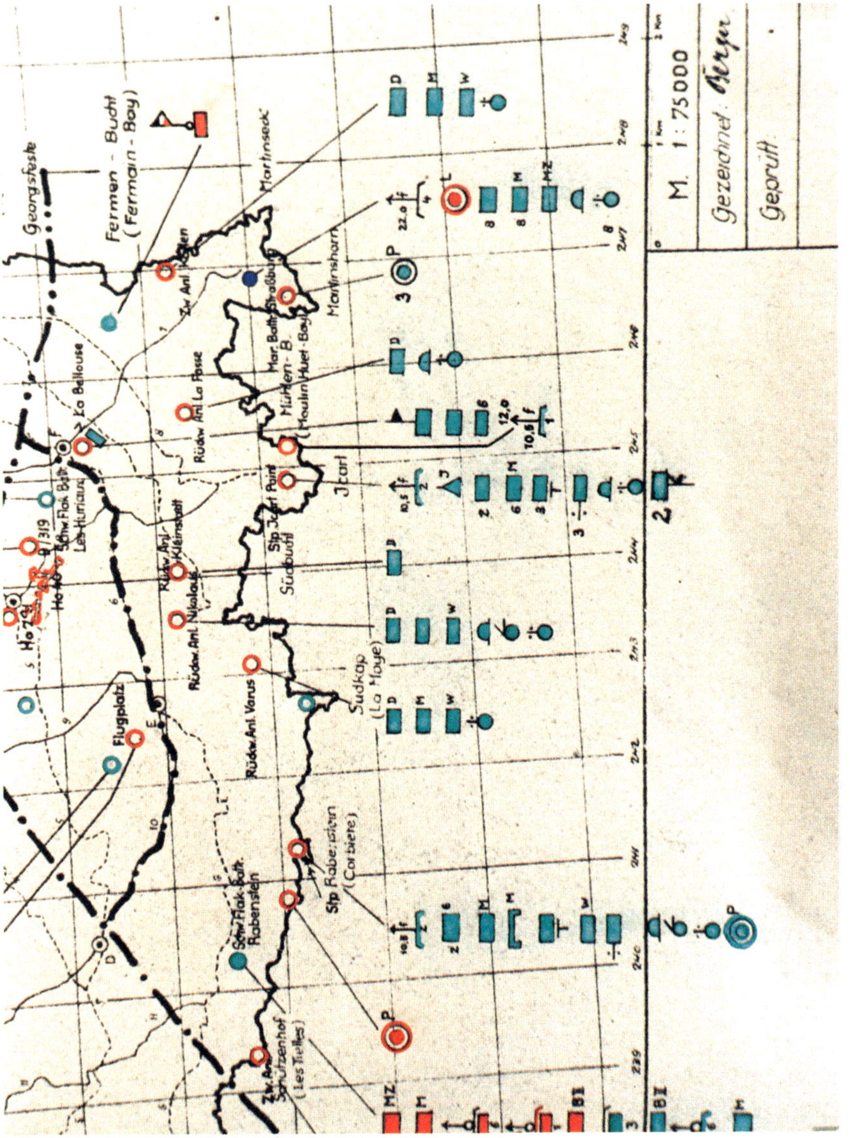

PLp	RCp	Description of contents
19	115	Waffen-u.Besatzungs-Stärken auf den Kanalinseln nach stand vom 1.5.43, 1.11.43, 1.7.44: (Weapons and garrison strength of the Channel Islands as at 1st May and 1st November, 1943 and 1st July, 1944. A very interesting statistical summary.)
20	ni	Bttrn.auf den Inseln stand 1.9.44: (Batteries on the Islands, a table of all the sites, number of artillery pieces, ranges and type of emplacement in which they are located.)
21	ni	As for 1.3.20, but details of coastal defence pieces, anti-tank weapons and quantities of concrete used in cubic metres (613,000cbm in total – 272,000 in Guernsey, 255,000 in Jersey and 86,000 in Alderney.)
22	ni	Gliederung der auf den Kanalinseln einges, Artillerie, Landeabw. Gesch.u.Heeres-Flak. (Table showing organisation for the Channel Islands; Artillery, coastal defence weaponry and Army A.A.)
ni	116	Feuerzusammenfassungen Guernsey, map at 1.25000 scale (Map showing concentrated fire zones for various bays around Guernsey, which would be used in the event of a landing, together with code names and units designated to fire.)
23	ni	Von der 319 I.D., sind im Nov. 1942 auf den Brit. Kanalinseln zu verpflegen . . . . (Table showing the logistical commitments of 319 Infantry Division in November 1942 on the Channel Islands. These include such items as food, fuel and ammunition.)
24	114	Alderney, map at 1:25000 scale: (Details as 1.3.7.)
25	ni	Infanterie-einsatz Alderney, map at 1:25000 scale.
26	ni	Artillerie-einsatz Alderney, map at 1:25000 scale.
27	ni	Flak-einsatz Alderney, map at 1:25000 scale.
28	109	Diagram illustrating a dozen of the pilotage marks to be found in local waters and obstructions in silhouette, each indicated at various states of the tide.

As might be expected, the above section 1.3. has provided information for many articles in the *Occupation Review*, such as 'German ground radar in the Channel Islands' by Alan G. Hobbs (1988 p.53) and 'The 319 Infantry Division in the Channel Islands' by Michael Ginns (No. 19 p.40). There are many more facts and figures still to be published from this section.

SECTION 1.4

Festungsmäßige Bauten (Permanent fortifications)

PLp	RCp	Description of contents
missing	76	Colour drawings of railway mounted trucks, loaded next to what appears to be a gravel crushing unit, entitled 'Festungsmäßige Bauten'. (An "artist's impression" - not a specific site)

PLp	RCp	Description of contents
M	77	Übersicht über die Betonleistungen, Guernsey, map at
i		1:50,000 scale: (Summary of concrete output. Graphs
s		detailing quantities of concrete used between Jan. 1941 and Aug. 1944.)
s	78	K.V.U. Guernsey-Ost, map at 1:75000 scale: (War survey
i		document Guernsey-East. Plots every weapon and
n		individual bunker employed in this sector.)
g	79	K.V.U. Guernsey-Nord, map at 1:75000 scale (Sector north)
	80	K.V.U. Guernsey-West, map at 1:75000 scale (Sector west)
	81	K.V.U Guernsey-Süd-(Mitte), map at 1:75000 scale (Sector south/centre)
H	82	Divisionsgefechtsstand: (Divisional battle headquarters)
e	83	Regimentsgefechtsstand: (Regimental battle headquarters)
f	84	Nachrichtenstand: (Signal post)
t	85	Kleinstunterstand für 6 (9) Mann: (Small bunker for 6 (9) men)
	86	Gruppenunterstand: (Group bunker)
	87	Unterstand für 60cm Scheinwerfer mit Bereitschaftsraum: (Bunker for 60cm searchlight with alert room.)
	88	Munitions-Unterstand: (Ammunition bunker)
	89	Stand für M19: (Emplacement for M19 [5cm mortar])
	90	Stand mit 6 Schartenturm und 3.7 K.w.k.(f): (Bunker with 6 embrasure turret and French 37mm tank gun.)
	91	Stand für 4, 7 Pak (t). (Bunker for Czech 47mm anti-tank gun.)
	92	Stand für 4, 7 Pak (t): (Bunker for Czech 47mm anti-tank gun.)
	93	Stand für 4, 7 Pak (t) u.M.G. in Panzermauer rechts Flankierend: (Bunker for Czech 47mm anti-tank gun and Machine Gun in anti-tank wall right flanking position.)
	94	Schartenstand für Gesch. auf mittl. Sockellafette ohne Nebenräume (120°): (Embrasured emplacement for guns on pedestal mount (120°) without ancillary accommodation.)
	95	Photographs qty.4 (in RC). (Views of Ho.12 and Ho.40, 1 photo missing.)
	96	Fold out colour print of St. Saviours Church entitled 'Hohlgang 12 Munition'. (Tunnel 12 Ammunition)
	97	Fold out colour print showing the layout of Ho.12 below St. Saviours Church.
	98	Fold out colour print of hillside in St. Andrews, entitled 'Hohlgang 40 Lazarett'. (Tunnel 40 Military Hospital)
	99	Fold out colour print showing the layout of Ho.40 and uses of each annex.

Note: RCp 82./94. inclusive, each contain a scale plan of the bunker and colour drawing of the exterior.

Many of the above have been used in books on the occupation, one in particular being 'The War in the Channel Islands Then and Now' by W. G. Ramsey. Nearly all the locations illustrated can still be seen today.

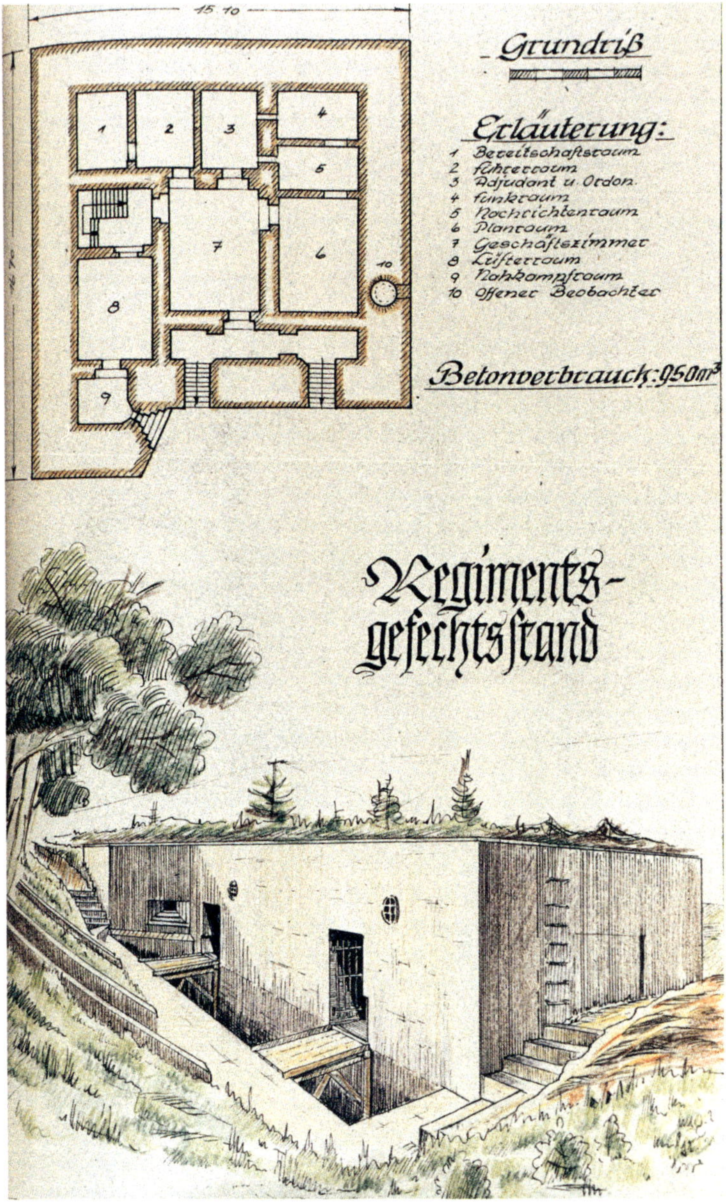

The two storey fortress standard battle headquarters of Infantry Regiment 584, responsible for the northern half of Guernsey, on a hill-top site at Beau Séjour, St Peter Port.

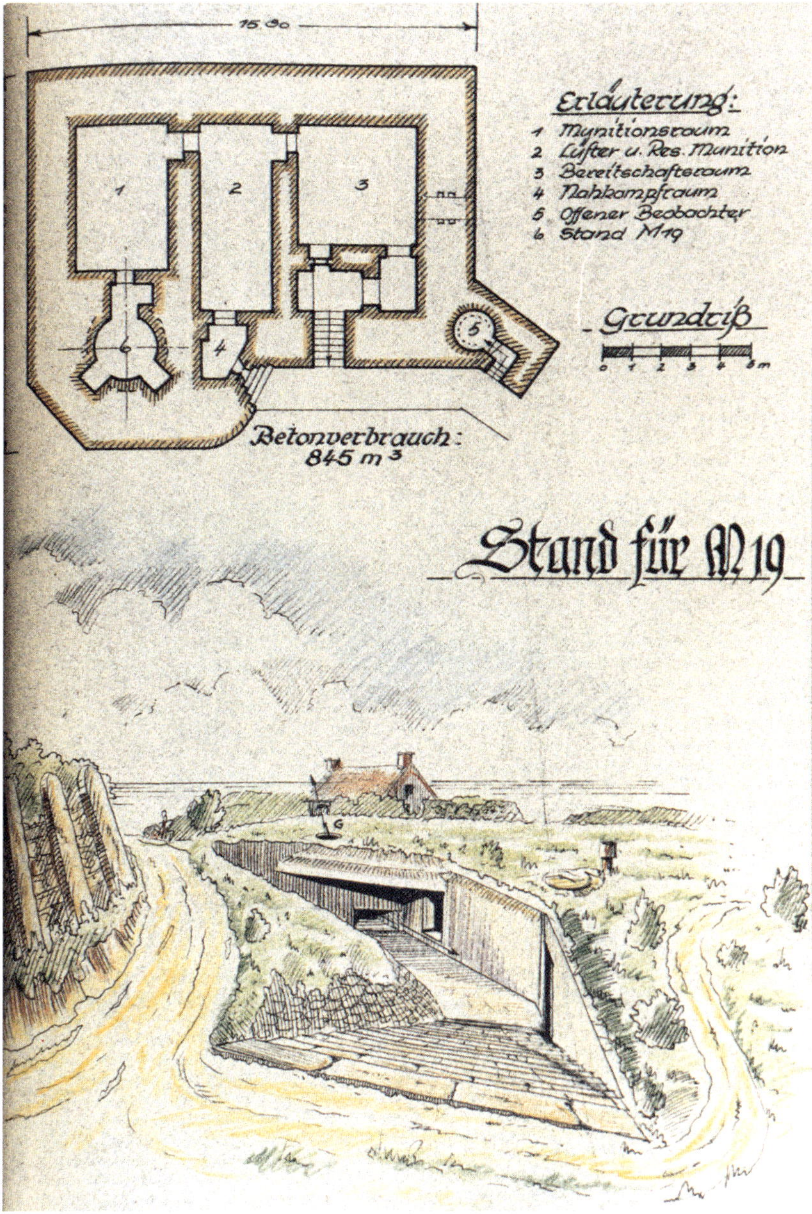

M19 automatic 5cm mortar bunker at Fort Saumarez; the boundary wall of Le Creux ès Faies Dolmen is visible to the left.

SECTION 2.1

Eingesetzte Waffen (Operational Weaponry)

PLp	RCp	Description of contents
m	55	Colour drawing of flak guns firing from concrete
i		emplacements entitled 'In der Festung Guernsey
s		Eingesetzte Waffen'.
s	56	Photographs qty. 4 (in RC)
i	57	Photographs qty. 3 (in RC)
n	58	Photographs qty. 3 (in RC) (1 photo missing)
g	59	Photographs qty. 5 (in RC) (1 photo missing)
	60	Photographs qty. 4 (in RC)
h	61	Photographs qty. 5 (in RC) (1 photo missing)
e	62	Photographs qty. 5 (in RC)
f	63	Photographs qty. 5 (in RC)
t	64	Photographs qty. 3 (in RC) (1 photo missing)
	65	Photographs qty. 4 (in RC)
	66	Photographs qty. 4 (in RC)
	67	Photographs qty. 6 (in RC)
	68	Photographs qty. 6 (in RC)

A very interesting series of pictures. They show a wide range of subjects such as uses for grenades, flame-throwers and mines, machine guns in a variety of roles, motorised units, anti-tank units, tanks, interiors of bunkers and day to day routines in flak units. A number of these photographs have been used extensively, but some still await publication.

SECTION 2.2

Batterie Mirus (Battery Mirus)

PLp	RCp	Description of contents
TP	69	Colour drawing of one of the Mirus emplacements entitled 'Batterie Mirus'.
1	70	Die Geschichte der 30, 5cm Rohre in Batterie 'Mirus'. (Essay on the history of the 30, 5cm gun barrels in Battery Mirus).
2	ni	Batterie Mirus, map at 1:5000 scale (Battery plan showing layout of the guns, local defence positions and ancillary works).
3	71	Photographs qty. 4 (in PL), qty. 3 (in RC)
4	72	Photographs qty. 4 (in PL), qty. 3 (in RC)
5	73	Photographs qty. 4 (in PL), qty. 6 (in RC)
6	74	Photographs qty. 4 (in PL), qty. 4 (in RC)
7	75	Photographs qty. 4 (in PL), qty. 5 (in RC)
8	ni	Photographs qty. 4 (in PL)
9	ni	Photographs qty. 3 (in PL)
10	ni	Photographs qty. 4 (in PL)

PLp	RCp	Description of contents
11	ni	Photographs qty. 4 (in PL)
12	ni	Photographs qty. 4 (in PL)
13	ni	Geschütz der Batterie Mirus (Colour drawing showing an oblique view of one of the emplacements, including the internal layout of the annexed rooms.)

Virtually all this material has been published, with probably the best publication being 'Mirus, The Making of a Battery' by Colin Partridge and J. Wallbridge. The pictures themselves show general views of the guns, daily routines, internal equipment of the command bunker, and battery radar.

SECTION 2.3

Einsatz der Artillerie (Operational Artillery)

PLp	RCp	Description of contents
m	117	Colour drawing showing an artillery piece firing entitled
i		'Einsatz der Artillerie'.
s	118	1. Kampfauftrag der Küstenartillerie im allgemeinen.
s		(Combat duties of the coastal artillery in general.)
i		2. Kampfauftrag der Divisionsartillerie im allgemeinen.
n		(Combat duties of the divisional artillery in
g		general.)
		3. Vorbereitete Feuer. (Preparedness to fire.)
h	119/	4. Kampfaufträge der einzelnen Batterien, abgesehen vom
e	121	allgemeinen Kampfauftrag. (Gives details of the
f		combat duties for each individual battery, except for
t		those outlined in previous sections on RCp. 118.)

This is a very small and apparently incomplete section, but it does contain a few pieces of useful information. However, this pales into insignificance when compared to the similar section in *Festung Jersey,* which goes into great detail, such as to include detailed plans of each battery site.

SECTION 2.4

Einsatz der Flak-Artillerie (Operational anti-aircraft artillery)

PLp	RCp	Description of contents
missing heft	122	Map entitled 'Flak-Guernsey' showing the locations of all the flak units in Guernsey from 2cm to 8.8cm. Also included are six larger scale maps on the same page, showing the main flak battery layouts for the 8.8cm sites, drawn to approximately 1:5000 scale.

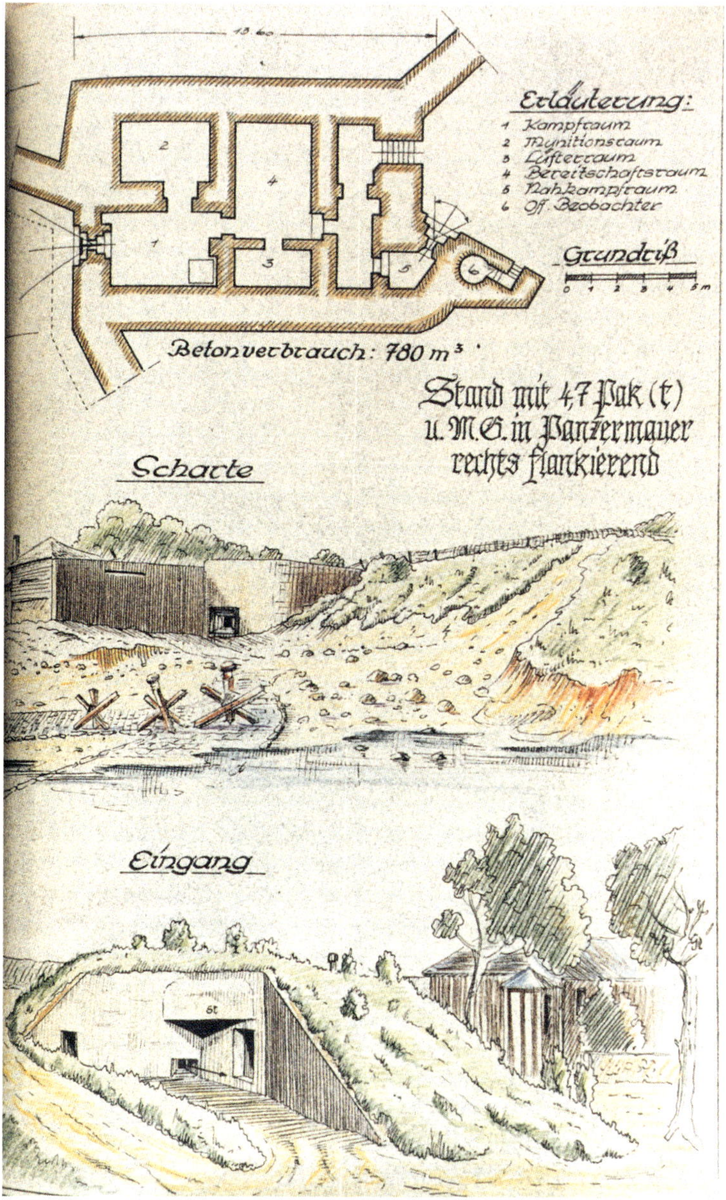

4.7cm Skoda anti-tank gun bunker, right flanking, at Fort Saumarez. (Five out of the thirteen bunkers illustrated in this section are plainly located on the Fort Saumarez headland).

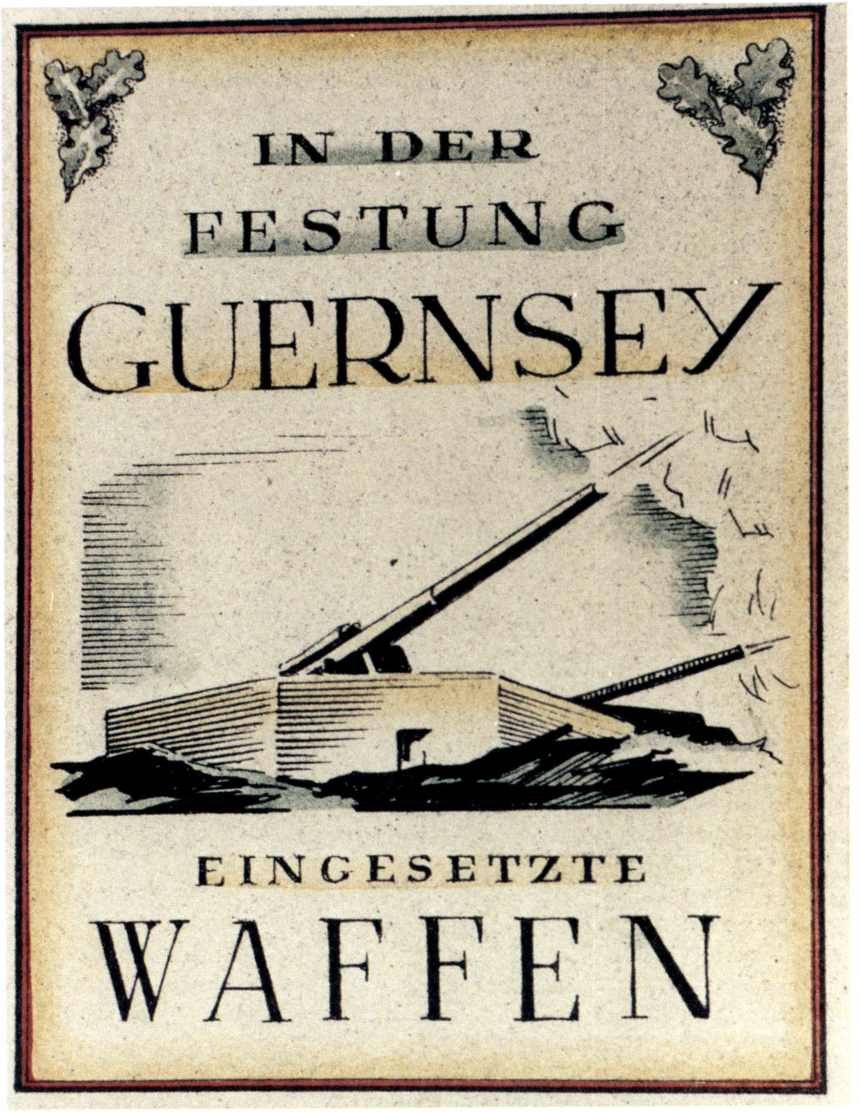

Frontispiece of the section entitled Eingesetzte Waffen or Weapons Emplaced. Insofar as this represents a specific site rather than a general impression of artillery en barbette, it may be based on Batterie Gneisenau at La Ruette des Fries, Cobo, Guernsey, where four 15cm K18 guns were mounted until August, 1944, when they were moved to Jersey to counter the new threat posed by the Allies on the adjacent French mainland.

A one page section. There are, however, two or three blank pages which follow which I have not indexed, but it does raise the question, did they intend to insert some photographs?

SOME CONCLUDING COMMENTS

The above analysis reveals that the Royal Court edition is reasonably intact, yet as it was made up from carbon copies of the pages used in the Priaulx Library edition, it does pose one or two questions. The first must be, just how much more information was there, when the Germans first completed the Priaulx Library edition? The remaining sections of the Priaulx copy indeed hold a far greater wealth of information, yet when it was presented to the Library some sections were already missing, and other portions have subsequently disappeared.

It seems strange that there are only two copies in existence. Usually most things seem to get done in triplicate, so are there other copies? This could well be the case as I have seen other documents which would indicate this may be possible. Do you, the reader, know of any more? I would like more details if possible. If you have any questions, then I will do my best to help you.

SOURCES, REFERENCES AND ACKNOWLEDGEMENTS:

Festung Guernsey: Royal Court Library & Priaulx Library, Guernsey

A Shopkeeper at Sea by R. Palmer: C.I.C. Review, Guernsey 1985

Atlantic Wall Typology by R. Rolf: AMA Uitgeverij, Beetsterzwaag NL, 1988

Channel Islands Occupation Reviews - various: Guernsey & Jersey, 1973/91

German Army Uniforms and Insignia 1933-1945 by B. L. Davis: Arms and Armour Press, London 1977

German Military Dictionary by U. S. War Department, 1944: reprint, Lancer Militaria, Arkansas USA, 1992

Handbook on German Military Forces by U.S. War Department (TM-E 30-451): reprint, U.S. Government Printing Office, Washington, 1945

Mirus, The Making of a Battery by C. Partridge & J. Wallbridge: The Ampersand Press, Alderney, 1983

Normandy 1944 by S. Badsey: Osprey Publishing Ltd., London, 1990

Small Arms, Artillery and Special Weapons of the Third Reich by T. Gander & P. Chamberlain: Macdonald and Jane's Publishers Ltd., London 1978

The Military Eitzen by K. H. Eitzen: Verlag E. S. Mittler & Sohn, Herford, Germany, 1988

The von Aufsess Occupation Diary by Baron von Aufsess: Phillimore & Co. Ltd., Chichester, 1985

The War in the Channel Islands, Then and Now by W. G. Ramsey: Battle of Britain Prints International Ltd., London 1981

ACKNOWLEDGEMENTS

My thanks are due to the Royal Court and the Priaulx Library, and their respective librarians, for their assistance in the carrying out of the research for this article, and for permitting material to be reproduced.

The illustrations are all from the Royal Court edition, save for those on pages 11 and 13.

HOW TO JOIN THE CHANNEL ISLANDS OCCUPATION SOCIETY

Are you interested in joining the C.I.O.S.? Both Guernsey and Jersey have active branches, meetings being held throughout the year with an emphasis on outside excursions during the summer months, and film shows and talks in the winter. Members receive the annual Review and regular newsletters free, and have access to the Society's extensive documentary, sound, film and photographic archives. For those requiring further information or who are interested in joining the Society as resident or overseas members, please contact the secretaries of the respective branches.

Succeeding pages:

Two card covers. Cards were issued in various colours, according to the material the printer had in stock.

A typical identity card, that issued to the writer's father. This card bears five stamps; the number of the card; the signature of the then President of the Controlling Committee, Ambrose Sherwill; the swastika applied when the card was scrutinised by FK 515 prior to issue in November 1940; the seal in red of the Registrar-General of Identifications (i.e. H.M. Greffier) over the photograph when that was added to the card on 29 August 1941; and finally that of Barclays Bank Limited, applied when the card holder changed the permitted quantity of Reichsmarks into Sterling after Liberation in 1945.

IDENTITY CARD
IDENTITAETSKARTE
Star Typ.

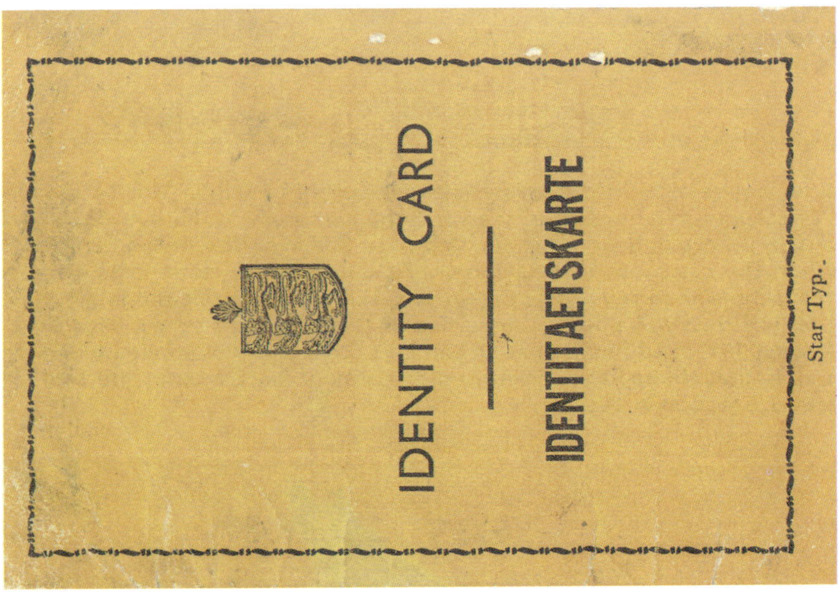
IDENTITY CARD
IDENTITAETSKARTE
Star Typ.

No. 20162 L

The holder of this Card is / Inhaber dieser Karte ist: TOUGH CLIFFORD HENRY

Residing at / Wohnhaft: Knette Braye St Martins

Born on the / Geboren am: 15 11 1904 at / in: Catel Guernsey

PARTICULARS—NÄHERE ANGA

M ... Single, Married, Widow or Widower

Verheiratet ... Ledig, verheiratet, verwitwet

Brown ... Colour of Hair

Braun ... Farbe des Haares

Grey ... Colour of Eyes

Grau ... Farbe der Augen

None

Kein

C. H. Tough

Tough

Controlling Committee of the States of Guernsey.

Feldkommandantur, Nebenstelle Guernsey.

THE IDENTITY CARD SYSTEM IN OCCUPIED GUERNSEY

Ken Tough

A compulsory identity card, complete with photograph, has been advocated in recent years as a means of discouraging fraud and impersonation and assisting in law enforcement generally. Identity cards are widely used in continental Europe. This article describes Guernsey's experience of such a system, when throughout almost five years of enemy occupation, all adult civilians had to carry such a card. This requirement was imposed by the German authorities when, shortly after their invasion in 1940, they discovered to their acute embarrassment that they had no sure means of establishing the identity of any given civilian, and this at a time when an indeterminate number of British agents were believed to be at large in the Island.

On 29th July, 1940, the States of Guernsey held a census of the civilian population; 23,981 people were found to have remained to face the occupation. There was at that time no system of national registration in force in the Island, although the States Insurance Authority, responsible for social security, held records of the insured population and compiled estimates of population trends for actuarial purposes. If a census is a snapshot of the population taken at five or ten year intervals, registration with identity cards can be likened to a continuous moving picture recording a mass of personal detail over time. A census is essentially a numbers exercise in which the facts about individuals, gathered on a confidential basis, are merely a means to a statistical end. Registration, by contrast, is primarily concerned with details on individuals, and the central records form an enormous personal database, from which any desired analysis can be carried out, subject only to the practical limitations of manual searching through, in the case of Guernsey, more than twenty-two thousand application forms. The Germans, as will be described later, had of course ulterior motives in their choice of the personal data required to be declared; on the other hand universal registration had obvious merits for civilian policing and rationing purposes.

The spur to introduce identity cards was provided, all unwittingly, by the British War Office. Between 6th July and 4th September, 1940, a total of five British officers were sent on clandestine missions to Guernsey to gather information about the enemy forces. One, Captain John Parker, was apprehended immediately on landing; as for the remainder, in each case arrangements for them to be picked up and returned to England went awry; inevitably in such a densely populated

Island, the prolonged stay of these agents, who were all Guernseymen, became known to the Germans although they were unable to trace them individually. Ultimately all four had to give themselves up, and their friends and relations were interrogated and in some cases temporarily imprisoned in France. The Germans soon discovered that they had no ready means of checking the identity of civilians to distinguish between bona fide residents and suspected British agents, especially if the latter were themselves Islanders.

Early in October, 1940, therefore, the newly appointed Commander-in-Chief in the Islands, Colonel Graf von Schmettow, mindful of the security problem posed by a large enemy population with no compulsory identity documents, directed the civilian authorities in both Guernsey and Jersey to register all persons over the age of 14 and issue them with identity cards. By this time two further agents, Second Lieutenants Philip Martel and Desmond Mulholland, had already given themselves up, but rumours persisted that more were still at large. On 12th October, 1940, the Royal Court of Guernsey made an Ordinance empowering the Controlling Committee to set up a registration and identity card system. One the same day there appeared in the *Guernsey Evening Press* a remarkable exchange of letters between Major Bandelow, the German Kommandant in Guernsey, and Ambrose Sherwill, the President of the Controlling Committee, the executive 'cabinet' which had been set up by the States of Guernsey in June, 1940. In his letter, drafted by Sherwill – a prominent Guernsey lawyer who held the post of His Majesty's Procureur (Attorney-General) – Bandelow confirmed that any British soldiers in hiding in Guernsey who gave themselves up would be treated as prisoners of war. In the event six British servicemen, who had been on leave in the Island when the Germans invaded and had lain low ever since, duly surrendered, in addition to the two remaining agents, Captain Hubert Nicolle and Second Lieutenant James Symes.

Details of the identity card system were published on 19th October, 1940, in the Registration and Identification of Persons (Bailiwick of Guernsey) Order 1940 made by the Controlling Committee. This required every inhabitant aged 14 years or over, regardless of nationality but excluding 'members of the uniformed forces of the German Reich', to obtain and carry at all times an identity card and to produce it for inspection on the request of a German serviceman in uniform, a Parish Constable, Douzenier or Police Officer.

Throughout the Occupation the Island authorities endeavoured to maintain civilian government, in accordance with their own best judgment and with the advice of the British government in the last hectic days before the invasion, while accepting the necessity to co-exist with the occupying forces.

C-72-23.

REGISTRATION FORM.

Denoting Letter and Number of Place of Issue to be entered here

62

Two copies of this Form must be completed by every person.
If you are in doubt as to how to complete this Form, the Constable or a Douzenier of your Parish will help you.

Evacuated.

For Official use only.

No. 10301

(*a*) Surname in block letters followed by Christian names. (*a*) STOCKWELL
ALICK, STRONACH

A1843 28.8.45 12 NEW ST. ST. P. PORT.

(*b*) Ordinary Postal address, including Parish (*b*) ~~KINGSTON,~~
VER~~TERUE, VALE~~

(*c*) Date of Birth (*c*) 17:10:1873

(*d*) Place of Birth (*d*) Weymouth

(*e*) Nationality* (*e*) British

(*f*) Occupation (*f*) NIL, other than Registrar Gen. of Identification

(*g*) Single, married, widow or widower (*g*) MARRIED

(*h*) Colour of hair (*h*) GREY

(*i*) Colour of eyes (*i*) BROWN.

(*j*) Any physical peculiarities, such as a scar, limp, etc.

Stockwell

(*k*) Have you served in any of His Britannic Majesty's Armed Forces? If so, write R.N., R.N.R., Army, R.A.F., Royal Guernsey Militia, or as is appropriate and give your rank on retirement and the date of retirement

(*l*) Are you on a Reserve of Officers of His Britannic Majesty's Armed Forces? If so, state which Reserve

(*m*) Are you, not being on a Reserve of Officers, on the Reserve of any of His Britannic Majesty's Armed Forces? If so, state which Reserve. (*m*) No.

*_As regards question (e), if you are a person possessing dual nationality, give both nationalities._

Extract from the registration form of Major Alick Stockwell, a retired regular soldier, who set up the identity card system in 1940. It records his deportation in 1942 with the laconic overstamp in red "Evacuated to Germany", and his subsequent return on 21 August, 1945. (The Greffe).

In relation to the Registration Order of 1940 this was reflected in the paradox that it provided that any contravention of the Order would be punishable both under German penal law by German military tribunal and before the civil courts in Guernsey as an offence against the Defence Regulations (Guernsey), 1939. It is ironic that one of the express purposes of those Regulations, made under the Emergency Powers (Guernsey Defence) Order 1939, an Order of His Majesty in Council, was to assist in "the efficient prosecution of any war in which His Majesty may be engaged".

The Controlling Committee appointed Major Alick Stockwell as the first Registrar-General of Identifications. Born in England in 1873, Stockwell retired from the army in 1934. He had superintended the emergency census held in July, 1940 and had assisted in the organisation of the milk rationing scheme. His office was in the Ladies' College building at La Couperderie. In each of the ten Guernsey parishes the Constables were appointed as Registrars; in Sark this role was given to the Seneschal; in respect of Alderney, where only a handful of civilians remained, the Registrar-General was to liaise with the German military authorities in carrying out his duties. Reliance on voluntary parish officials was an integral part of the system, as indeed it was of Island government in general during the Occupation. Every application for an identity card had to be witnessed and countersigned by a Constable or Douzenier of the relevant parish; application forms had to be completed in duplicate, with one set being held by the Parish Registrar and the other being forwarded to the Registrar-General to be incorporated in the overall Bailiwick Register.

In accordance with German directions, the application form required each applicant to state his or her full name, address, date and place of birth, nationality, occupation, marital status, colour of eyes and hair and any physical peculiarities such as a scar, limp etc. In addition, applicants had to state whether or not they had ever served in the British armed forces, whether they or any near relative were on a reserve of officers and whether they had any near relations actually serving in the British armed forces. They were not however required to specify the unit or last known whereabouts of any such relation. From the forms submitted to him the Registrar-General had to draw up lists of everyone who had disclosed any such connections with the armed forces of the Crown; the German motive in making this requirement was to become clear two years later when persons were selected for deportation to Germany.

60,000 copies of the application form were printed by the *Guernsey Star* at their printing works in the Bordage, and registration of Islanders duly began on 24th October, 1940. In parish halls, douzaine rooms and parish schools throughout the Island, parish officials were soon at work scrutinising application forms; J. C. Sauvary, Douzenier of St Sampson's, spent a busy week in the Church Schools at Grandes Maisons Road and noted in his diary that "I have looked into more ladies' eyes this week than I ever did in all my life! Had I been colour blind I might have got out of the job!". The delegation of this task to the parishes ensured that as many people as possible could be identified by a responsible official who would then countersign the application form.

The completed identity cards were issued during the week beginning 25th November, 1940; applicants were required to collect them from the parish centre where they had handed in their forms the previous month and sign the card in the presence of a parish official who could vouch for them. Even in the close-knit parish communities of occupied Guernsey there were some who were not known to their parish officials, and they were advised to attend "in the company of some better known person".

The identity card was printed in English and German and gave the following details: number of card, holder's full names, address, date and place of birth, marital status, colour of eyes and hair and any physical peculiarities. Each card bore the stamped signature of the President of the Controlling Committee; Sherwill was removed from all his public offices by the Germans in January, 1941 and was subsequently deported to Germany in February, 1943, but because by the end of 1940 the vast majority of cards had already been issued, his signature, that of one who was very much persona non grata with the Germans, continued to authenticate those cards for the rest of the occupation. Finally, prior to being sent to the parish centres for issue, the cards were sent in batches to the Feldkommandantur 515 ("FK 515") at Grange Lodge where a plain circular stamp was applied, featuring the all-too familiar spread winged eagle above a laurelled swastika.

Although the Germans, through their Military Government Officers in FK 515, took a keen interest in the efficient operation of the identity card system set up at their behest, they did not hold a duplicate set of application forms; both the parish registers and the central register remained in civilian custody. However, in addition to inspecting all cards prior to issue, they required the Registrar-General to liaise with them and to make information available on request.

At the end of 1940 Stockwell asked to be relieved of his duties as Registrar-General of Identifications and the post was given to His Majesty's Greffier, who was of course already Registrar-General of Births, Marriages and Deaths. The system had been successfully implemented; by 6th January, 1941, the date of the transfer, 22,103 identity cards had been issued, including 396 to residents of Sark and seven to civilians in Alderney, whose forms had been checked and countersigned by the Inselkommandant and forwarded by him to Guernsey.

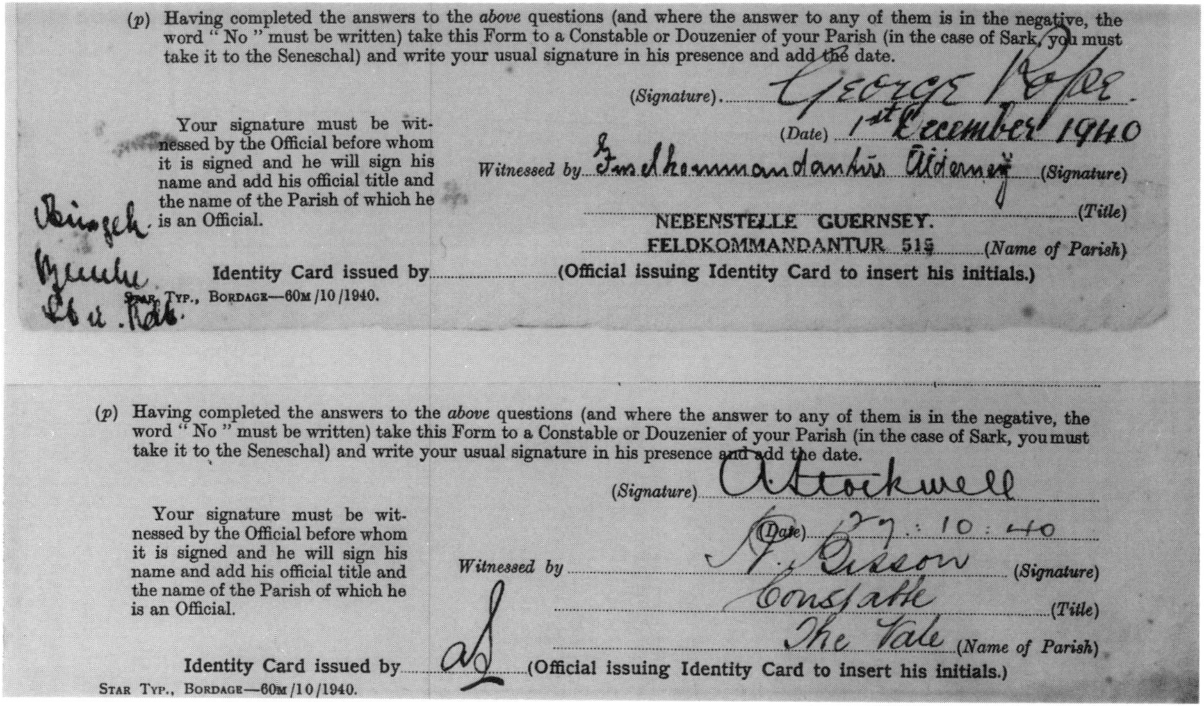

(p) Having completed the answers to the *above* questions (and where the answer to any of them is in the negative, the word "No" must be written) take this Form to a Constable or Douzenier of your Parish (in the case of Sark, you must take it to the Seneschal) and write your usual signature in his presence and add the date.

Your signature must be witnessed by the Official before whom it is signed and he will sign his name and add his official title and the name of the Parish of which he is an Official.

(*Signature*) George Pope.

(*Date*) 1st December 1940

Witnessed by Inselkommandantur Alderney (*Signature*)

NEBENSTELLE GUERNSEY. (*Title*)

FELDKOMMANDANTUR 515 (*Name of Parish*)

Identity Card issued by .... (Official issuing Identity Card to insert his initials.)

Star Typ., Bordage—60m/10/1940.

(p) Having completed the answers to the *above* questions (and where the answer to any of them is in the negative, the word "No" must be written) take this Form to a Constable or Douzenier of your Parish (in the case of Sark, you must take it to the Seneschal) and write your usual signature in his presence and add the date.

Your signature must be witnessed by the Official before whom it is signed and he will sign his name and add his official title and the name of the Parish of which he is an Official.

(*Signature*) A Stockwell

(*Date*) 27 : 10 : 40

Witnessed by .... (*Signature*)

Constable (*Title*)

The Vale (*Name of Parish*)

Identity Card issued by .... (Official issuing Identity Card to insert his initials.)

Star Typ., Bordage—60m/10/1940.

Signatures on registration forms had to be witnessed by a responsible parish official. The seven civilians in Alderney had their forms countersigned by the Inselkommandant in that island and forwarded to Guernsey by the German authorities. They differ from Guernsey and Sark forms in not subsequently having photographs attached. By way of illustration extracts are reproduced here from the registration forms of Stockwell himself, and of George Pope, a pilot and fisherman in Alderney. (The Greffe).

Photographs did not form part of the original scheme, and neither the registration forms nor the identity cards issued in 1940 were designed for photographs to be attached to them. However, as early as 5th January, 1941, when Stockwell called at Grange Lodge to report to Dr. Brosch of FK515 prior to relinquishing his post, he was told that the Germans were considering the addition of photographs to all cards already issued.

Eventually, on 14th March, 1941, detailed instructions for the extension of the system to include photographs were issued by Dr. Reffler of FK515. They were to be of passport type, 5 x 6 centimetres in size, and were to be affixed to the right hand inside page of each card, in the section set aside for further particulars. Three copies were to be provided of each photograph, which was not to be more than three years old; in addition to the copy to be attached to the card itself, one copy was to be attached to each of the registration forms held in the parish and central registries respectively. In order to harmonise with the paralled system in Jersey details of dependent children under fourteen years of age were to be entered on the father's registration form, or, in the case of illegitimate children, on their mother's form. The maiden name was to be added to the forms of married or divorced women and widows. On 17th May, 1941, the Royal Court made an Ordinance requiring all holders of identity cards to provide such photographs or to submit to be photographed under arrangements to be made by the Controlling Committee. By contrast with the original Ordinance of 12th October, 1940, this Ordinance expressly stated in the preamble that it was made following the decision of the German Kommandant that photographs be attached to identity cards. Any failure to comply with this Ordinance or any Order made under it would be punishable as an offence against the Defence Regulations (Guernsey), 1939, but not, it would seem, under German penal law also as in the case of the original Ordinance.

On 19th May, 1941, Guernsey newspapers published details of what the *Evening Press* described as "the biggest photographical undertaking ever seen in Guernsey"; some 20,000 photographs were to be taken and a total of 60,000 prints made. Charles Toms, the well known *Evening Press* staff photographer, would be in charge, assisted by a regular team of two and by other cameramen as needed. The filming would be carried out parish by parish and would be free of charge – a feature which was calculated to appeal to all true Guernseymen then as now. The times and places at which the filming was to take place were published on 21st May, 1941, in an Order by the Controlling Committee.

This operation provided a unique, comprehensive portrait of the entire population over fourteen years of age. Everyone, even the blind and disabled, had to submit to be photographed. Persons confined to home or hospital could apply for exemption, but they were forbidden

Statement of Identity Cards issued prior to 6th January, 1941.

Parish	Cards issued			Cards cancelled	Valid Cards in hands of population:
	from	to	Total		Total
St.Peter Port	1	7895	7895	70	7825
St.Peter's	8501	9509	1009	6	1003
Vale	9701	12876	3176	43	3133
St.Sampson's	13401	16095	2695	15	2680
Castel	16531	18998	2468	20	2448
St.Martin's	(19101 (21101	20872 21600	1772) 500)	15	2257
St.Saviour's	(21601 (22376	22353 22400	753) 25)	2	776
St.Andrew's	22601	23453	853	5	848
Torteval	23701	24139	439	4	435
Forest	24201	24509	309	3	306
Sark	24701	25100	400	4	396
			22294		22107
less Cards Nos.7894, 7895, 9508 & 9509 (as per List No.35 of 4.1.41.), these cards having been prepared but not yet issued			4	-	4
Totals:			22290	187	22103

Copies to Nebenstelle Guernsey der
Feldkommandantur 515.
The President of the Controlling Committee
of the States of Guernsey.
The Registrar General of Identifications.

By the end of 1940 the system was complete, and Stockwell submitted this statement of cards issued to date when he relinquished his post in January 1941. Note that the schedule is copied to Feldkommandantur 515 (the German Civil Affairs Unit at Grange Lodge Hotel), the President of the Controlling Committee, and to Stockwell's successor as Registrar-General of Identifications. (Island Archives Service).

thereafter to appear in any public place without first having obtained an identity card complete with photograph. In practice such exemptions were few, and the registration records contain many portraits of people who might not otherwise have been photographed, such as members of religious orders, persons in extreme old age, the bedridden in hospital, 'imbeciles' etc.

Work began in St. Andrew's on 26th May, 1941 and concluded in St. Peter Port on 6th August, 1941. 21,884 people were filmed during the intervening period as the team of cameramen and registration officials toured Guernsey and Sark. H. M. Greffier, Alfred Roussel, was in overall charge as Registrar-General of Identifications, and his Deputy, James Le Page, was directly responsible for organising the operation. The numbers to be photographed ranged from some 8,000 in St. Peter Port to just 470 in Torteval.

The filming was done by daylight, on weekdays between 11.00 a.m. and 7.00 p.m., making the most of the light evenings provided by the German-imposed double summer time. It generally took place at parish halls or douzaine rooms; in the larger parishes different centres were used on successive days, as in St Sampson's where Brookdale Nursery, Kenilworth Vineries and Fountain Lodge Vineries were the venues on 30th June, 1st July, and 2nd and 4th July respectively. Eight days were allocated for filming in St Peter Port, six at Candie Gardens and two at the Plateau Mignot. Each photograph was given a number, which was displayed in a wooden frame to the subject's left, rather like hymn numbers in church. The number was preceded by the customary parish letters, as used on cycle tax receipts etc., anti-clockwise around the Island from "A" for St Peter Port to "K" for St Andrew's, omitting "J". Thus every identity card photograph could be authenticated by its letter/number combination; it should however be noted that this number bore no relation to the number allocated to each identity card.

This exercise in mass portraiture was described in Island newspapers as "Guernsey's photo-census" and gave journalists a much-needed human interest story at a time when they were chronically short of news which they were permitted by the German censor to print. Through the summer months of 1941 the filming of Mr. and Mrs. Guernsey vied for readers' attention with communiques from Berlin on the progress of the war in Russia and elsewhere, which the Germans required to be given prominence on the front pages.

593 people were photographed in St Andrew's on the opening day of the "photo-census"; it was a fine day and, in the words of the *Evening Press* reporter on 27th May, "most of the 'shooting' was done in the open air at the side of the Church Hall". No doubt the censor was familiar with English photographic jargon and was not concerned by this reference to a rural fusillade. The quality of sub-editorial humour

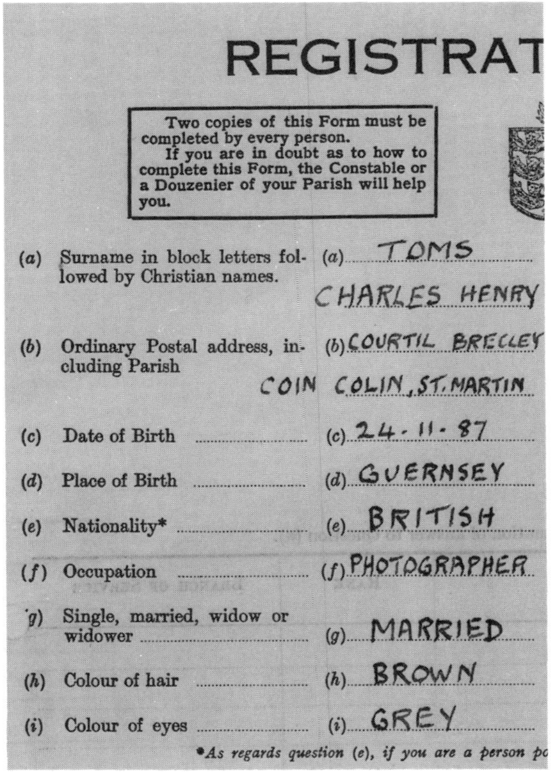

REGISTRAT

> Two copies of this Form must be completed by every person.
> If you are in doubt as to how to complete this Form, the Constable or a Douzenier of your Parish will help you.

(*a*) Surname in block letters followed by Christian names. (*a*) TOMS CHARLES HENRY

(*b*) Ordinary Postal address, including Parish (*b*) COURTIL BRECLEY COIN COLIN, ST. MARTIN

(*c*) Date of Birth .... (*c*) 24 - 11 - 87

(*d*) Place of Birth .... (*d*) GUERNSEY

(*e*) Nationality* .... (*e*) BRITISH

(*f*) Occupation .... (*f*) PHOTOGRAPHER

(*g*) Single, married, widow or widower .... (*g*) MARRIED

(*h*) Colour of hair .... (*h*) BROWN

(*i*) Colour of eyes .... (*i*) GREY

**As regards question (e), if you are a person po*

Extract from the registration form of Charles H. Toms, photographer, and enlargement of his identity card photograph. (The Greffe).

was plainly unaffected by the trials of enemy occupation – on 12th June a report on an especially productive filming session in St Martin's attracted the headline "They made it 'snappy'."

Photographs were taken at up to one hundred per hour; at the same time forms were handed out to be filled in by parents with dependent children under fourteen years of age. The photographer was supported by assistants who produced another camera with a fresh film as the preceding film was finished; a travelling dark room was parked nearby, ready to process the exposed films. The German authorities ensured that sufficient photographic materials were made available; these were of course in short supply after a year of occupation, and the civilian photographers took the opportunity discreetly to replenish their stocks for later use.

After six hectic weeks the photographic team deserved a break, and on 9th July they began a "working holiday" in Sark so that, to quote the *Evening Press* report on 23rd June, "the inhabitants can be 'shot' in their natural surroundings". Charles Toms and three colleagues set up their studio at Major Breen's empty house at La Ville Roussel; Breen, a former British Press Attaché in pre-war Berlin, had evacuated to England immediately before the occupation. 370 Sarkees were photographed that day, and the following day private visits were made to the homes of the elderly and infirm. The oldest to be photographed was 93 year old Mrs Guille of Little Sark, and the youngest her great-granddaughter Miss Margaret Guille, who would not be 14 until 27th July.

Once three prints had been made from each negative, cardholders were required to attend at their respective parish centres with their identity card; there they had to write their surname on each of the three prints, one of which was attached to the identity card and authenticated with the red circular stamp of the Registrar-General of Identifications; the other two prints were attached to the registration forms completed by each card holder in 1940 and filed in the central and parish registers respectively. This procedure began in St Saviour's on 18th August, and was completed in St Peter Port on 17th October, 1941.

The identity card system was now essentially complete. It was however vital that the information recorded be kept up to date. The original Order of 19th October, 1940, required every person forthwith to report to his Parish Registrar any change of address, occupation or marital status, and that Registrar had to forward that information to the Registrar-General so that the latter could amend the relevant files and, if necessary, issue a fresh identity card. Similarly any person over the age of fourteen years who had just arrived in, or was about to leave, the Island, had to report that fact to his Parish Registrar for onward transmission to the Registrar-General. The loss, or finding, of an

The "photo-census" in progress in the summer of 1941. Charles Toms is shown photographing a subject, with reference number displayed on an easel. An assistant photographer, A. J. Keates, (pastrycook of Hauteville and Fountain Street, St. Peter Port) looks on. (Carel Toms). Messrs. Toms and Keates in a moment of relaxation at Candie Gardens outdoor "studio" – the balcony east of the bandstand. (Carel Toms).

identity card had to be reported. On the death of a card holder the next of kin had to deliver the deceased's identity card to the Parish Registrar. As was to be expected, immediate compliance was not universal, and on 12th December, 1940, Stockwell, with the approval and possibly at the instigation of Dr. Reffler of FK515, published a formal notice in *La Gazette Officielle* in the Island newspapers reminding the public of the above provisions and emphasising that all such reports had to be made to the appropriate Parish Registrar and not directly to the Registrar-General at the Ladies' College. In a similar notice dated 20th October, 1941, the Bailiff, at the request of FK515, drew attention to the fact that any non-German person staying the night in a hotel, guest house etc. must deposit his identity card and immigration permit with the landlord who, together with the traveller, was responsible for complying with the registration regulations.

Changes of address, marital status and the like were noted on the relevant registration forms in both the central and parish registers by the Registrar-General or his staff. When a card holder died his form was transferred to the appropriate deceased file in the central registry. An ominous red stamp with the laconic message "Evacuated to Germany" was applied to the still current registration forms of the rather more than 900 Island residents deported from September, 1942, onwards. As children reached the age of fourteen years they were photographed and issued with their own identity card.

The primary purpose of the system was of course to identify civilians in their day to day contact with German security personnel, not only when stopped in suspicious circumstances such as when abroad after curfew, but also when passing checkpoints at the harbours or in military zones elsewhere in the Island as authorised workers, local residents or farmers attending to their crops or cattle. The cards also assisted the civilian authorities in the rationing of food and other essentials; as the occupation wore on and shortages grew, the decision whether or not to grant a card to an individual became almost a matter of life or death.

By the spring of 1944 possession of a civilian identity card virtually acquired the status of unofficial "naturalisation" or acceptance as a bona fide British resident. A number of foreign workers, mainly of French, Dutch and Spanish origin, who had been brought to Guernsey as part of the impressed Organisation Todt work force which reached a peak of 5,100 in May 1943, had remained in the Island after their OT employers had been withdrawn to France in the winter of 1943-1944, having formed relationships with, and in several instances having married, Guernsey girls. The plight of these men was now desperate; the Germans repudiated any responsibility for them as they were no longer in their employ; on the other hand the Island authorities were reluctant to grant their pleas to be granted a civilian identity card, and thus access

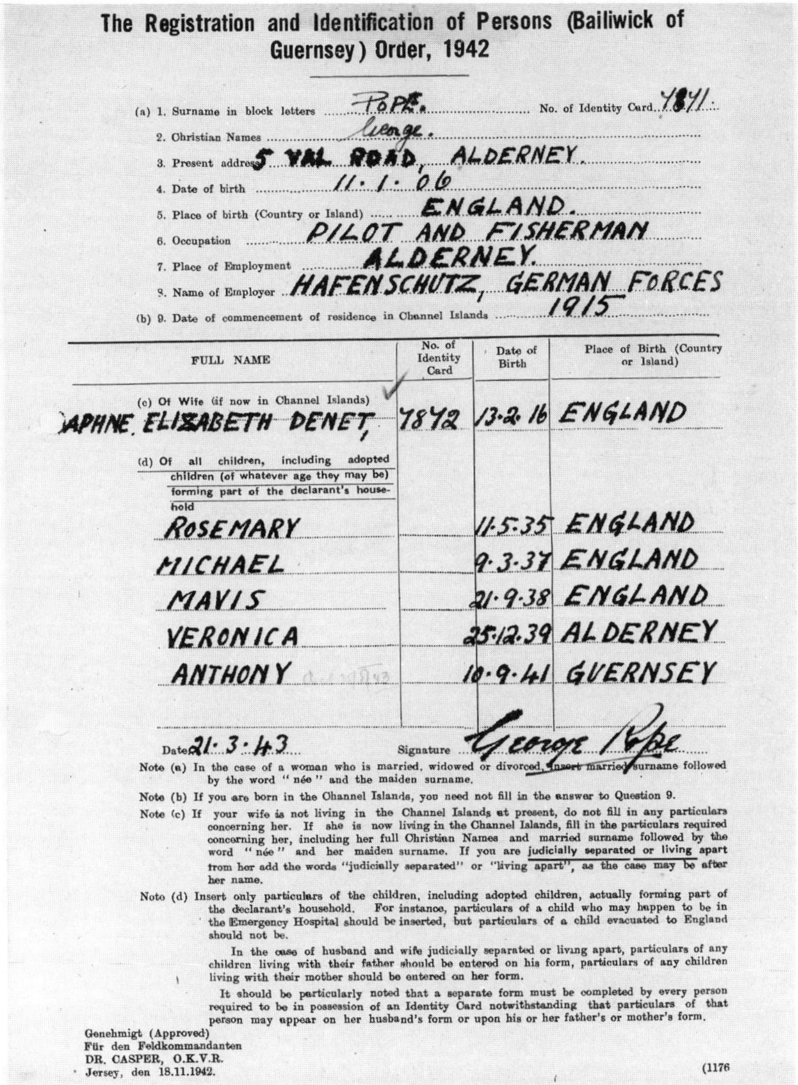

The Registration and Identification of Persons (Bailiwick of Guernsey) Order, 1942

(a) 1. Surname in block letters ....POPE........ No. of Identity Card ....7841....

2. Christian Names ....George........

3. Present address ....5 VAL ROAD, ALDERNEY....

4. Date of birth ....11·1·06........

5. Place of birth (Country or Island) ....ENGLAND........

6. Occupation ....PILOT AND FISHERMAN........

7. Place of Employment ....ALDERNEY........

8. Name of Employer ....HAFENSCHUTZ, GERMAN FORCES....

(b) 9. Date of commencement of residence in Channel Islands ....1915........

FULL NAME	No. of Identity Card	Date of Birth	Place of Birth (Country or Island)
(c) Of Wife (if now in Channel Islands)			
DAPHNE ELIZABETH DENET	7842	13·2·16	ENGLAND
(d) Of all children, including adopted children (of whatever age they may be) forming part of the declarant's household			
ROSEMARY		11·5·35	ENGLAND
MICHAEL		9·3·37	ENGLAND
MAVIS		21·9·38	ENGLAND
VERONICA		25·12·39	ALDERNEY
ANTHONY		10·9·41	GUERNSEY

Date 21·3·43 Signature George Pope

Note (a) In the case of a woman who is married, widowed or divorced, insert married surname followed by the word "née" and the maiden surname.

Note (b) If you are born in the Channel Islands, you need not fill in the answer to Question 9.

Note (c) If your wife is not living in the Channel Islands at present, do not fill in any particulars concerning her. If she is now living in the Channel Islands, fill in the particulars required concerning her, including her full Christian Names and married surname followed by the word "née" and her maiden surname. If you are judicially separated or living apart from her add the words "judicially separated" or "living apart", as the case may be after her name.

Note (d) Insert only particulars of the children, including adopted children, actually forming part of the declarant's household. For instance, particulars of a child who may happen to be in the Emergency Hospital should be inserted, but particulars of a child evacuated to England should not be.

In the case of husband and wife judicially separated or living apart, particulars of any children living with their father should be entered on his form, particulars of any children living with their mother should be entered on her form.

It should be particularly noted that a separate form must be completed by every person required to be in possession of an Identity Card notwithstanding that particulars of that person may appear on her husband's form or upon his or her father's or mother's form.

Genehmigt (Approved)
Für den Feldkommandanten
DR. CASPER, O.K.V.R.
Jersey, den 18.11.1942.

(1176

The Register of Identifications had to be kept up to date. The 1942 form requiring additional information about dependents was posted to George Pope in Alderney for completion and returned to the Greffe, Guernsey. The printed note at the foot is a reminder that the identity card system was closely supervised by FK 515. "O.K.V.R." is an abbreviation for Oberkriegsverwaltungsrat or senior military government officer. (The Greffe).

to civilian rations, at a time when the civilian population was facing starvation, partly as a result of the requisition of civilian food stocks by the German military.

The problem became acute early in January, 1945, with the arrival of prisoner of war type parcels provided by the International Committee of the Red Cross; these were strictly for the benefit of the British population only, and not for the Germans or their auxiliaries.

On 10th January, Jurat the Reverend John Leale, who had succeeded Ambrose Sherwill as President of the Controlling Committee in December, 1940, wrote to the Bailiff of Jersey with a view to establishing a consistent policy; put shortly, should foreigners who had married Guernsey girls be issued with civilian identity cards and thus given the right to receive Red Cross parcels? There were about 40 such cases in the Island, of whom half had already been granted cards and the rest were now applying. Unfortunately the relevant Controlling Committee file (1/1/2 at the Island Archives) does not contain any reply to this letter.

Strict enforcement of the identity card regulations was constantly urged by the German authorities. Civilians who were stopped by German patrols and found not to be in possession of a card were fined by the military; those apprehended by the Island police were brought before the Police Court. On 13th January, 1943, Brosch complained at the large number of civilians who were having to be prosecuted for losing their identity cards; such loss was generally due to gross negligence and the usual fine of 5 shillings with the alternative of 48 hours imprisonment was inadequate. What did the Controlling Committee propose to do about this? Leale forwarded this letter to Sherwill for his comments. The latter, who had been allowed by the Germans to resume his functions as H. M. Procureur in July, 1942, and was in that capacity responsible for all criminal prosecutions in the civil courts, replied that although he appreciated the misgivings of the German authorities, in many cases the culprits were in humble circumstances and if a larger fine were imposed the penalty would almost certainly fall on the family rather than just on the loser of the card. "Life is hard for many people these days and, in particular, one does not wish to be so harsh that children will be deprived of food". Leale duly copied this response to Brosch. On 15th January, 1944, Dr Kratzer of FK515 wrote complaining that Feldgendarmerie officers often found that identity cards were in bad condition, and that sometimes the attached photographs had been lost.

The identity card regulations continued in force after the liberation of the Islands on 9th May, 1945. Former evacuees returning home from the United Kingdom had to hand in their National Registration Identity Cards and apply for a Guernsey card; however they were not required to submit photographs with their application. The vast majority of identity cards in use still of course bore the swastika stamp. On 31st July, 1945, *The Star* newspaper carried a report of 25 persons prosecuted before the Police Court for cycling without lights: "Several of the delinquents had left their identity cards at home, and were fined 1/- extra. Mr Ernest Despointes, of Houmet Lane, Vale, who was one of these, told the Magistrate "I thought these cards and their Nazi eagle were things of the past". "Mr Despointes' patriotic objection was finally met on 17th December, 1945, when the Occupation identity card system was formally wound up.

EPILOGUE – NATIONAL REGISTRATION AND THE ELECTORAL ROLL 1945-1952

As soon as possible after Liberation the United Kingdom system of rationing was introduced in the Islands and it was a logical further step to bring in National Registration Identity Cards on the U.K. model. Effective from December, 1945, these cards carried no photographs of the holder, were issued to all – i.e. not just to those of 14 years of age and over – and were not of course bilingual. The word "Guernsey" was over-printed in red on the face of each card. National Registration had been set up in the U.K. in 1939 under the General Register Office, based on an enumeration of the population carried out on 29th September of that year using machinery devised for the 1941 Census which was cancelled because of the war. The database thus created was then kept up to date and used to assist the Ministry of Food in the issue of ration books and the Ministry of Labour and National Service in enforcing registration for conscription etc.

In June, 1946, a Committee of the Privy Council was appointed to enquire into reforms in the constitution and procedure of the States of Jersey and Guernsey. This issue had been the subject of political debate in the Islands since the Liberation. In their wide-ranging Report, published in March, 1947, the Committee referred to criticism in both Islands of the way in which the electoral roll was compiled. In each Island the Parish Constables, responsible for the roll in their respective parishes, discriminated between persons eligible for the franchise who were ratepayers and those who were not. The former were automatically included in the electoral roll; the latter had to apply each year to the Constables to be inscribed on the roll. As a result women voters, and other non-householders, tended to be under-represented on the electoral roll. The Committee recommended that for all public elections there should be a published electoral roll compiled on a uniform basis without discriminating between ratepayers and non-rate payers.

In Guernsey this was achieved by simply adopting the National Register as the basis for the electoral roll in each parish. Thus the

National Register, successor to the Occupation identity card system, created as a by-product a fully comprehensive electoral roll. As a result there were 28,317 names on the electoral roll at the first general election for People's Deputies, in December, 1948, following the coming into force of the Reform (Guernsey) Law, 1948. In addition identity cards were checked to prevent anyone casting two votes; in all parishes where there was more than one polling station voters were required to present their identity card so that it could be stamped to show they had cast their vote.

In the event this system came to an end after only two triennial elections, when in November, 1952, the States resolved to end National Registration the following month, in line with the United Kingdom authorities. However one prescient member opposed that proposal; Douzaine Representative J. P. Warren spoke in favour of retaining National Registration while food rationing was in force. Moreover, he argued that, in relation to housing control, identity cards could be used to establish the bona fides of people resident in Guernsey, and some people had already found them useful to prove their identity when travelling outside the Island.

NOTE ON SOURCES

This article is based primarily upon a study of the Central Register of Identifications held at the Greffe, Guernsey. This consists of some 200 files containing more than 22,000 original application forms, each signed by the cardholder and bearing his or her photograph. Applications for identity cards submitted between the Liberation and December, 1945, are also in the Greffe archives, but did not have photographs affixed. The Central Register covered the whole Island, together with Alderney and Sark, and is arranged in aphabetical order. A complementary set of Parish Registers is held at the island Archives. These Registers provide a unique portrait of the people of Guernsey under enemy occupation. (By contrast, the files of the post-War National Register appear not to have survived.)

The other main sources are the files of the *Guernsey Evening Press* and *The Star*, and the original text of the relevant Ordinances of the Royal Court and Statutory Instruments, also held at the Greffe, and the Controlling Committee files on the identity card system, at the Island Archives. The generous assistance and hospitality of the Island Archivist, Hugh Lenfestey, and his Assistant, Bill Gallienne, is gratefully acknowledged.

The photographs of Charles Toms engaged on the 'photo-census' are published by kind permission of his son Carel, for access to whose rich collection – and memory – of Island images generations of writers on Guernsey have had cause to be grateful.

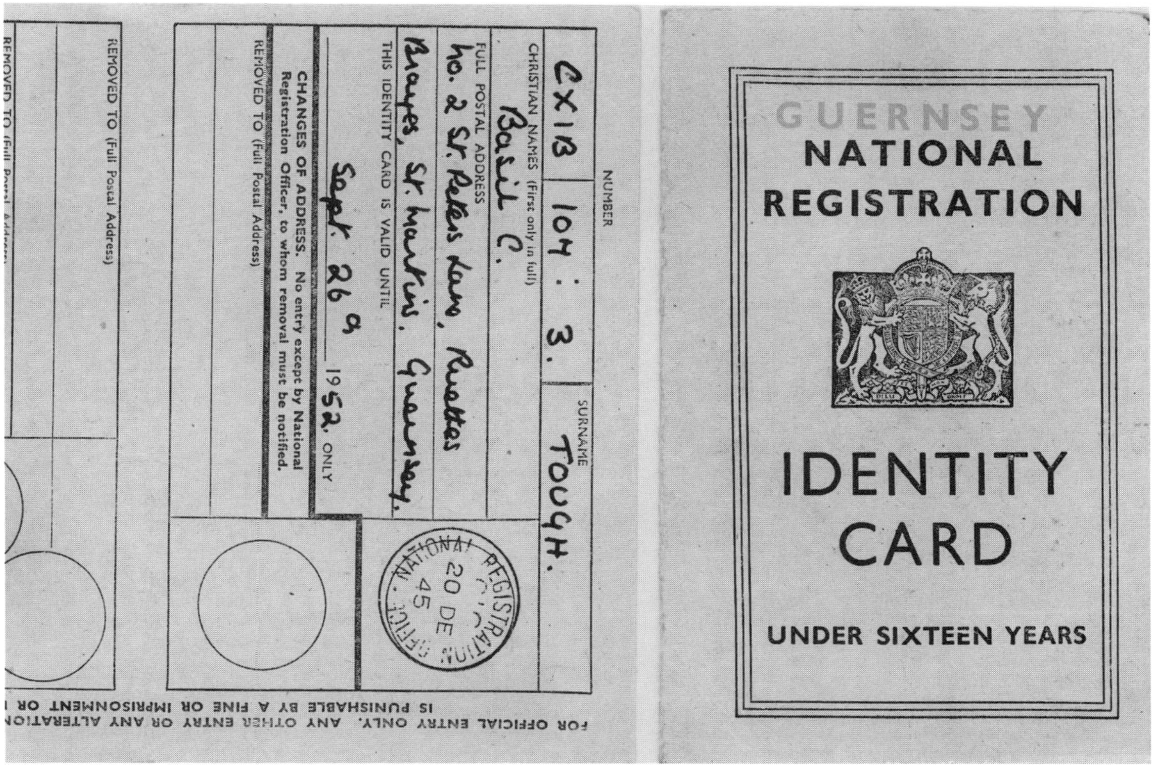
NUMBER
CXIB | 104 : 3.
SURNAME
TOUGH.
CHRISTIAN NAMES (First only in full)
Basil C.
FULL POSTAL ADDRESS
ho. 2 St. Peters Lane, Ruettes
Brayes, St. Martins. Guernsey.
THIS IDENTITY CARD IS VALID UNTIL
Sept. 26th 1952. ONLY
NATIONAL REGISTRATION OFFICE
20 DE 45
CHANGES OF ADDRESS. No entry except by National Registration Officer, to whom removal must be notified.
REMOVED TO (Full Postal Address)
REMOVED TO (Full Postal Address)
FOR OFFICIAL ENTRY ONLY. ANY OTHER ENTRY OR ANY ALTERATION IS PUNISHABLE BY A FINE OR IMPRISONMENT OR
GUERNSEY
NATIONAL
REGISTRATION
IDENTITY
CARD
UNDER SIXTEEN YEARS

A National Registration identity card, with "Guernsey" overprinted in red. Issued on 20 December 1945 when the Occupation identity cards were replaced.

GERMAN ROAD NUMBERING SYSTEMS
PART 1 - JERSEY

Michael Ginns & Colin Isherwood

The resident motoring population of both Guernsey and Jersey is all too familiar with the sight of a self-drive hire car stopped dead on the yellow line of a busy road junction while the driver and front seat passenger frantically scan the totally inadequate map with which they have been issued in an attempt to work out the route to the destination of their choice.

Any islander who looks, no matter how remotely, as if they perform an offical function (be it policeman, postman, milkman or dustman) is just as familiar with the plaintive cry "Excuse me! Could you tell me if we're on the right road for Bonney Newitt?" (variations can be Kwane/Booley Bay/Torty Val/Pleenmont etc.). While the less well bred will wind down their window and bawl "Hey, Jack! Are we O.K. for St. Breelaid's?" Ill mannered demands for directions from oafs such as these are best dealt with by telling them to carry straight on and turn at the next set of traffic lights – no matter in which direction they may be heading.

Holidaymakers who bring their own cars to the Channel Islands are usually better prepared and will be equipped with more informative maps than those issued with hire cars. However, insofar as Jersey is concerned, this type of map introduces another problem – road numbers! In the distant past (since the end of World War II admittedly, but in the distant past all the same) the then States of Jersey Main Roads Committee introduced a road numbering system for the island; this was based on the English system with all roads falling into an 'A', 'B', or 'C' category depending upon width and/or status, etc.

Local people totally ignore this system but to the lost car-borne holidaymaker it is a breath of home! A way out of all difficulties! And they eagerly ask, "Are we on the A6?" Or, "Will this take us to the B52?" Total bewilderment sets in when the equally baffled Jerseyman admits that he hasn't got a clue as to what the A6 is, or to where the B52 goes!

If these problems of direction route finding beset tourists who have a generally helpful resident local population to offer assistance, imagine if you can the plight of the German soldier in 1940, newly arrived in the island to which he has been posted. Completely lost and bewildered, driving on the wrong side of the road (driving on the right did not commence until 23 June, 1941, no matter what the television documentaries try to tell us), and a local population which, if not actually hostile, was distinctly truculent and, in any case, unable to speak German.

It is not surprising, therefore, that military planners had to put their heads together in order to produce a system of route finding which would be simple to follow and easy to apply. As in so many other facets of the German military systems in the Channel Islands, the chosen method of route indication varied considerably between Guernsey and Jersey and this difference was in part dictated by the road systems to be found in each island.

In the olden days Jersey's road system consisted of a network of narrow, deep, lanes on which two vehicles could scarcely pass side by side and which became nothing more than muddy ditches in periods of wet weather. However, in the early years of the 19th century the Governor of Jersey, General Don, caused ten broad military roads to be created. These fanned out like the spokes of a wheel from St. Helier so that the General's troops and artillery could gallop to any part of the island's coastline to repel threatened French landings.

These military roads have had a lasting effect in that they still form the basis of Jersey's main road system (the 'A' roads, if one dare mention such things?) and they are used by the island's bus routes which are numbered around the island in an anti-clockwise sequence, a method followed by the German Army with their road numbering schemes.

By late 1940 the occupying forces were beginning to dig in and defensive positions that had started out as rudimentary *Feldwache* (outposts) manned by a sentry with a rifle or, at best, by a couple of men with a machine gun (see the *C.I. Occupation Review, no 18,* pp.62 to79), were being consolidated with concrete and were slowly developing into what would eventually become full blown resistance nests or strongpoints.

By April, 1941, these early positions had been identified with numbers running around the island in an anti-clockwise sequence beginning at Fort Henry, Grouville Bay, on the island's east coast, as follows:-

1 – Fort Henry; 2 – Victoria Tower (Faldouet); 3 – Archirondel Tower; 4 – Fliquet Bay (guard for telephone cable to France); 5 – Rozel Fort; 6 – Bouley Bay; 7 – Bonne Nuit Bay; 8 – Grève de Lecq; 9 – Plemont (guard for telephone cable to Guernsey); 10 – Kempt Tower; St. Ouen's Bay; 11 – "Hi-de-Ho!", St. Ouen's Bay (now the Watersplash).

In order to assist the drivers of military vehicles or, indeed, bodies of marching troops, to arrive at their destination, arrows began to appear all over the island surmounted by the appropriate defensive position number. As such, of course, these were not road numbers but rather signposts pointing to a particular destination. The arrows and numbers were all painted in white on the nearest suitable wall. If some seemed a

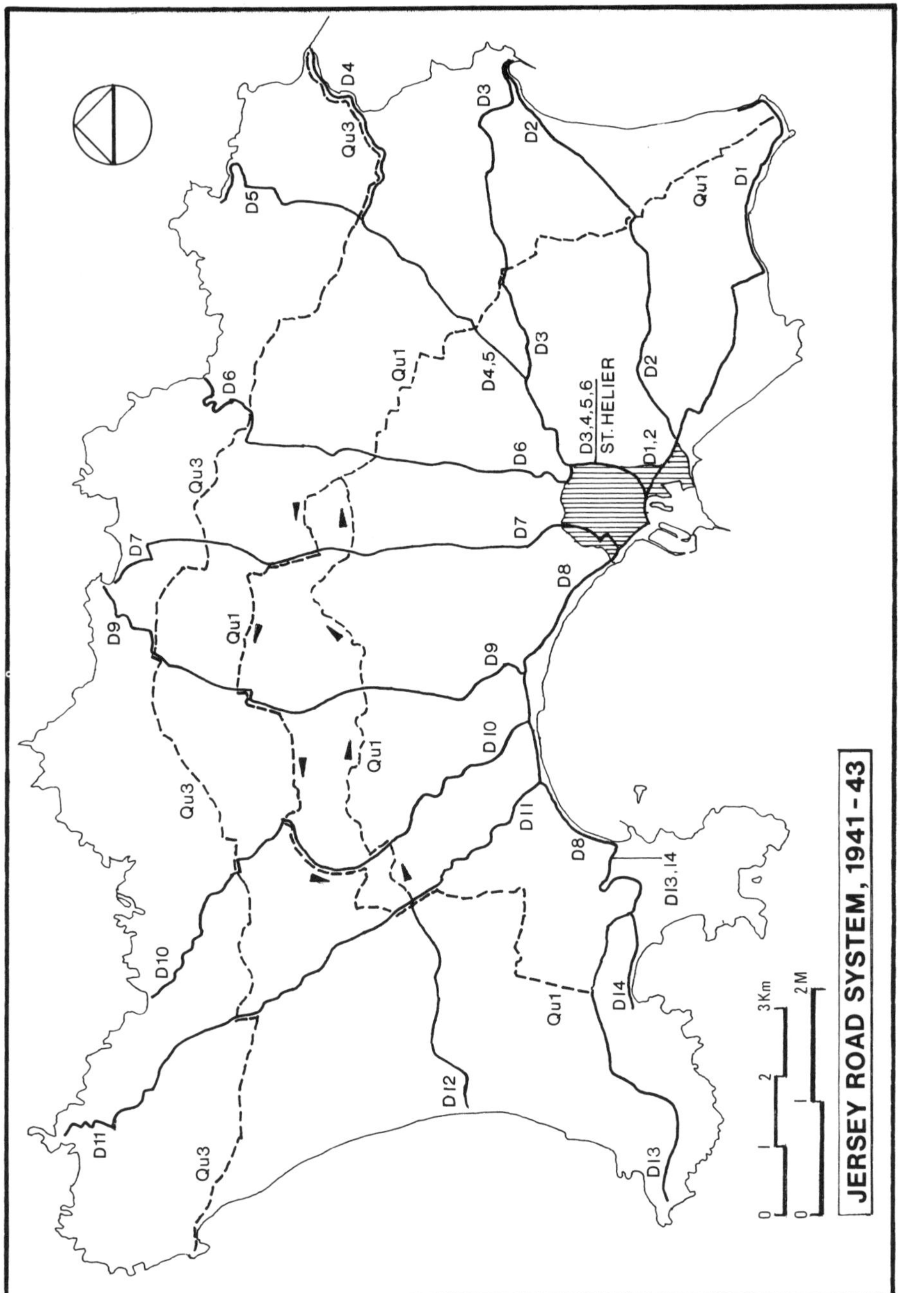

JERSEY ROAD SYSTEM, 1941 - 43

little crude, they at least had the advantage of being interference-proof and could not be turned around by mischievous youths who would derive much pleasure in diverting military traffic to the wrong part of the island.

The 1941 pattern of direction signs and the roads that they followed – where known from personal recollections, photographs, and what few faded examples that have survived – were as follows:-

1 and 2 – Don Road; Georgetown; Grouville Hill; Grouville Church; La Croix Cemetery – here the two separated, with 1 heading right towards Fort Henry and 2 carrying straight on to Gorey Pier, thence up Gorey Hill to Victoria Tower at Faldouet.

3, 4 and 5 – Colomberie, Mont Millais, Five Oaks – here 3 turned off via La Hougue Bie, Faldouet, and Les Landes Hill to end at Archirondel while 4 and 5 carried on via Maufant to St. Martin's Church and Rozel Manor; here, 4 turned right to Greencliff and Fliquet Bay, while 5 carried on to Rozel Bay.

It is almost certain that 6 proceeded via St. Saviour's Road, Springfield Road, and thence via Trinity Hill to Trinity Church, terminating at Bouley Bay and thus, without any firm evidence, it may be assumed that 7 to 11 followed the normal main roads to their respective defence positions.

As 1941 progressed and the German military presence increased, more positions were added to the coastal chain. It was obviously impossible to re-organise the entire numbering system every time a new defensive position opened up without causing chaos, so the later additions were given identification letters rather than numbers as, for example:- G = Gibraltar, or the round tower near St. Catherine's Cross Road; H = Le Hocq, the round tower at that point; R = La Rocque, or La Platte Rocque round tower; while, rather curiously, the slipway at Braye, St Ouen's Bay, became Q.

By the year 1942 the situation was becoming even more complicated with the addition of artillery and anti-aircraft batteries, many of them inland and well away from the coast and it obviously became impossible to enumerate each one individually. Thus was born the D road system.

D stood for *Durchgangsstrasse* or "Through Road" and these were numbered around the island in an anti-clockwise sequence, as follows:-

D1 – Colomberie, Don Road, Victoria Road, Platt Douet Road, St. Clement's Inner Road, Rue du Hocq and then along the Coast Road, terminating at Seymour Inn (La Rocque). Why this point was chosen as the outer destination is somewhat unclear.

D2 – Colomberie; Don Road; Longueville; Grouville Hill and Church; Route des Sablons to Gorey Pier.

D3, 4 & 5 – St. Saviour's Road & Hill, Five Oaks. Thence 3 via La Hougue Bie; Faldouet and Gorey Hill to Gorey Pier. 4 & 5 proceeded via La Grande Route de St. Martin to St. Martin's Church. Thence 4 to Verclut (St. Catherine's Breakwater) via Waverley Hill; and 5 to Rozel Bay via La Grande Route de Rozel.

D6 – St. Saviour's Road; Trinity Hill; La Route de Trinité; Trinity Church; La Rue és Picots; to Bouley Bay.

D7 – Rouge Bouillon; Queen's Road; Sion; Hautes Croix to Bonne Nuit.

D8 – West Park; St. Aubin's Road; La Route de la Haule; to St. Aubin.

D9 – Mont Felard; La Grande Route de St. Laurent; La Route de la Mare Ballam; La Rue de Mont Mado to Fremont Point.

D10 – Bel Royal; St. Peter's Valley; La Rue de la Vallée; St. Mary's Church; La Verte Rue; Le Rondin; Mont de Ste. Marie to Grève de Lecq.

D11 – Beaumont; Beaumont Hill; St. Peter's Church; Grande Route de St. Ouen; Route de Vinchelez; Portinfer to Plémont.

D12 – St. Peter's Church to Le Port (centre of St. Ouen's Bay) via Le Mont du Jubilé (Jubilee Hill).

D13 & 14 – St. Aubin; le Mont des Vaux to top of Mont Sohier; thence 13 to La Corbière via Route des Genets; Route Orange; Rue du Sud and Route de la Corbière; and 14 to St. Brelade's Bay via Mont Sohier.

The D roads were mainly signposted with wooden signs bearing black lettering on a white background. These were, on German orders, produced by the local signwriting firm of Le Brocq and Borny. All carried the letters B.d.B.K. (*Befehlshaber der Britischen Kanalinseln* = Commander of the British Channel Islands) in the bottom left hand corner. Signs at important junctions took the form of large boards, bearing the necessary information, and these were normally fixed firmly to walls or railings. The best known of these signs must be the example that was attached to the railings of no.1 Queen's Road and duly defaced by some bold islander with a "V" sign and the words BRITISH VICTORY IS CERTAIN. A photograph was taken and this must have appeared in practically every book that has been written about the Occupation (see Fig.3).

Lesser junctions were marked with signs painted on walls or with small wooden signs on posts driven into a handy hedge or roadside bank. The latter, however, had the disadvantage in that they were obvious targets for minor acts of sabotage as they were easily turned to point in the wrong direction. Whatever the ages of the perpetrators of these mild forms of sabotage against the Third Reich, it was always the local schoolchildren who got the blame and dire warnings would be read out at morning assemblies; coupled with the threat that any repetition would result in all males living in the immediate vicinity, between the ages of 18 and 55 being made to stand guard on all signposts during the hours of darkness.

Fig. 1: Today the States of Jersey Postal Headquarters stands behind this wall at the foot of Mont Millais, but in 1940 the wall displayed the direction signs to the early defensive positions in the Parish of St. Martin. (La Société Jersiaise).

Fig. 2: What was intended to be a casual snapshot of a soldier of the Luftwaffe standing outside "Quatre Bras" at the foot of St. Saviour's Hill has turned out to be a valuable historial record not only of a large sign of the D road system but also an obliterated arrow of the earlier, 1940, system. (La Société Jersiaise).

It was highly likely that the threat of a hefty parental clip around the ear if caught had more effect than the thought of Father standing shivering all night alongside a German road sign; but whatever the reason the practice waned after a while.

In tandem with the D road system, a number of cross, or diversionary routes around the islands was devised. In German, these were known as *Querstrassen*, abbreviated to Qu, which appeared on the appropriate signposts. The first to be put into operation was Qu 1 which meandered across the island from La Rocque Harbour, in the south-east corner, to Red Houses, St. Brelade, a distance of 14.2 miles (23 kilometres). The actual route was most convoluted, as follows:-

Qu 1 – from La Rocque Harbour, through the Parish of Grouville. Rue du Pont; Rue au Long; Rue des Cotils; Grouville Church; La Rigondaine; Le Catillon; Route de la Hougue Bie; through the Parishes of St. Saviour & Trinity: Rue des Pigneaux; La Fosse à l'Ecrivain; Rue de Chateau Clairval; Rue du Ponterrin; Victoria Village, La Commune; Rue au Bailli; Rue du Moulin du Ponterrin; Rue des Ifs; Rue de la Croix, to its junction with Rue des Haies; from here Qu 1 became one way and proceeded through Trinity, St. John and St. Lawrence via: Rue de Brabant; Rue Bechet; Grande Route de St. Jean; Chemin de Hérupe; Rue de la Scelleterie; Grande Route de St. Laurent; Le Passage; Six Rues; Verte Rue; Rue ès Boeufs; Chève Rue; Rue de la Vallée; through St. Peter and St. Brelade: Mont des Routeurs; Rue des Sapins; Grande Route de St. Pierre; St. Peter's Church; (here Qu 1 became two way again – for details of the route in an eastbound direction, see below); Rue des Landes; St. Peter's Arsenal; Route de Franc Fief; Pont du Val, Route de Quennevais; terminating at Red Houses.

The eastbound direction of Qu 1 over the one way section was:- St. Peter's Church; Route du Manoir; Mont du Presbytère; St. Peter's Valley; Mont de l'Ecole; Rue du Petit Aleval; Le Pissot; Rue de la Fontaine St Martin; Mont Perrine; Rue Milbraie; Mont de la Chesnée; Chemins des Moulins; Les Charrières Nicolle; Route de St. Jean; Rue des Saints Germains; Rue des Servais; Rue des Haies to its junction with Rue de la Croix near "Brabant". Here the route became two-way again.

If there was a Qu 2 it was never recorded as such, but a third cross-route was indeed introduced when the road numbering system was changed for a third time towards the end of 1942, or early in 1943, of which more in a moment.

Another known *Querstrasse* was Qu 3 which ran from Verclut Point (St. Catherine's Breakwater) in the north-east corner of the island, to L'Etacq, in the north-west, as follows:-

Qu 3 – St. Catherine's Breakwater; Waverley Hill; St. Martin's Church; Rue de la Croix au Maistre; St. Martin's Arsenal; Trinity Church; Rue du Presbytère; Route d'Ebenezer; Hautes Croix; Rue

Militaire; Route de Mont Mado; St. John's Church; Route de St. Jean; La Verte Rue; St. Mary's Church; Route de Ste. Marie; Les Chenolles; Chemin de l'Eglise; Rue de la Croix; Route de Vinchelez; Route du Marais; Mont Pinel, Route de l'Etacq; to l'Etacq.

The third road numbering system would appear to have been based on that of Guernsey because for the first time, a colour code was introduced. Under this system all the D roads were classed as "red roads" and simplified insofar as each route had its own number and did not share any stretch of road with another "red route"; for example, under the previous system D 3, 4 and 5 had all run along St. Saviour's Road and up St. Saviour's Hill to Five Oaks before separating. The prefix D was now dropped from the signboards themselves although it still appeared on the official German maps of the road system.

A second new feature was the introduction of an island ring road, the "blue" *Inselring*, while the former numbered Qu diversionary roads lost their numbers and were also colour coded. Hence the ertswhile Qu 1 became Qu "yellow", Qu 3 was incorporated into the "blue" *Inselring*; and a third diversionary route (which might have first been Qu 2) made its appearance as Qu "green".

The new "red roads" emanating from St. Helier did so from a town ring road which was not actually designated as such, but can be clearly picked out on surviving maps. This ran from the Weighbridge (Harbour) to West Park via Mulcaster Street; Hill Street; La Motte Street; St. Saviour's Road; Springfield Road; Rouge Bouillon; Undercliffe Road; New St. John's Road; Cheapside; and St. Aubin's Road, where it joined the *Inselring* at West Park.

The routeing for the new "red" D Roads was as follows:-

D1 – Colomberie; Don Road; Victoria Road; Plat Douet Road; St. Clement's Inner Road; Rue de Fauvic to Transvaal and a junction with the "blue" *Inselring*.

D2 – Georgetown; Bagot Road; Longueville; Grouville Hill; Rue à Don; to a junction with the "blue" *Inselring* on La Grande Route des Sablons.

D3 – Five Oaks; Prince's Tower Road; Route de la Hougue Bie; Faldouet; Gorey Hill to Gorey Pier.

D4 – Mont Millais; Grande Route de St. Martin to Maufant, where the road split with D4a proceeding to Rozel Bay via St. Martin's Church and La Grande Route de Rozel; and 4b proceeding to the same destination via Rue de Maufant; Pot du Rocher; Route des Cotes du Nord; and Le Mont de Rozel.

D5 – this was the old D6 from Trinity Road to Bouley Bay.

D6 – this was the old D7 from Queen's Road to Hautes Croix and Bonne Nuit Bay.

D7 – First Tower; Route de St. Jean (Mont Cochon); Le Huquet; Rue du Pont; Rue des Courts Champs; Route de Mont Mado; and Rue de Fremont to Fremont Point.

D8 – this was the old D9 from Mont Felard to St. John's Church; thence re-routed to Ronez Point via Rue de l'Etocquet.

D9 – this was the old D10 from Bel Royal to Grève de Lecq, via St. Peter's Valley, St. Mary's Church and Le Rondin.

D10 – this was the old D11 from Beaumont to Plémont, via Beaumont Hill and St. Peter's Church.

D11 – La Haule to Five Roads (St. Ouen) via Mont au Roux; Route du Coin; Route du Franc Fief; Pont du Val; Rue Carrée; Mont à la Brune; Rue de la Val de la Mare du Sud; Val de la Mare (Rue du Moulin); Mont Matthieu; Rue du Couvent; Rue de Grantez; Rue de Mahaut; and Le Hurel.

There were one or two curious features about this numbering system; firstly important places such as La Corbière and St. Brelade's Bay were not reached by any D road; and secondly, D11 was a most complicated route that served several headquarters which could have been far more easily reached by following D10 from St. Helier and turning left at the appropriate road junction.

All these new "red" D roads either commenced from/terminated at/or crossed over the "blue" *Inselring* which ran around the island as follows:-

St. Helier Harbour, Mount Bingham, Havre des Pas, St. Clement's Coast Road and La Grande Route des Sablons to Gorey Pier; here the road split into two with an outer leg proceeding via Anne Port, St. Catherine's Cross Roads, Rue du Moulin, Rue du Villot, Rue des Pelles, Route des Alleurs and Rue du Clos Fallu to St. Martin's Arsenal.

The inner leg proceeded from Gorey Pier via Gorey Hill, Grande Route de Faldouet, St. Martin's Church, Rue de la Croix au Maitre, Rue de la Maiterie, and Rue de Maufant to St. Martin's Arsenal where it re-joined the outer leg. Thence via La Profonde Rue to Trinity Church, Route d'Ebenezer, Hautes Croix, Routes des Issues, St. John's Church, Rue de St. Jean, Rue des Buttes, St. Mary's Church, Les Chenolles, and Route de l'Eglise to "La Chasse".

Here the *Inselring* split again with an outer leg proceeding via Rue de la Croix, Route de Trodez, Route de Millais, Rue de la Trape, Route des Landes, Mont du Vallet and Route de l'Etacq to the foot of Mont Pinel. The inner leg proceeded from "La Chasse" via Route Militaire, St. Ouen's Parish Hall, Route du Marais to the foot of Mont Pinel where it re-joined the outer leg.

Thence via Grande Route des Mielles (Five Mile Road), La Pulente, Rue de Sergenté, Route Orange, Route des Genets, Mont des Vaux, St. Aubin, Route de la Haule, Bel Royal, and Victoria Avenue back to St. Helier Harbour.

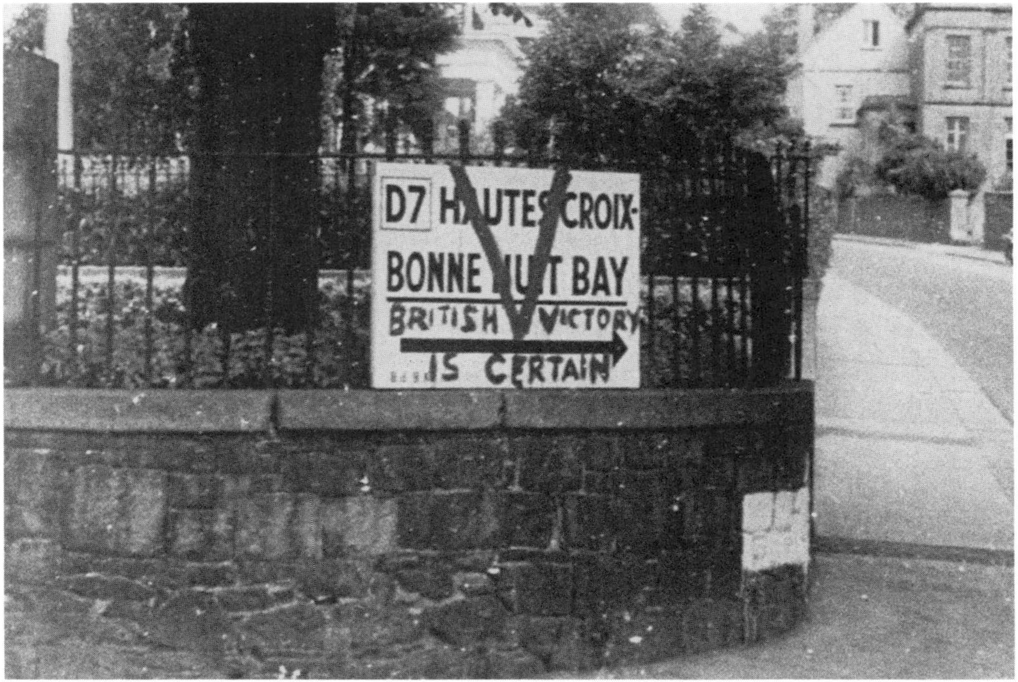

NOTICE

concerning "V" - Signs

"V" Signs have lately been discovered on the Traffic-Sign Posts of the German Army of Occupation in the following districts :

a) In Millbrook at the branching of the Rue du Gallet from Victoria Avenue.

b) In St. Ouen at the Crossroads, north of the Schoolhouse (Point 313).

The perpetrators have not been discovered.

I therefore decree that, as from 15.1.42 un ., and including 28.1.42, a guard must be set up both places by the Civil Population (excluding German or Italian Nationals) from the hours of 10 p.m. until 8 a.m. The guard is to be supplied by men of the age of 18 to the age of 55, who reside within a distance of 2 km of the mentioned places.

The guards are to be distinguished by the wearing of a blue and white armlet and must carry Passes supplied by me, together with their Identity Cards.

Any contravention of these duties will be punished according to the Order for the Protection from Sabotage given on 10.10.40 (VOBIF p. 108).

Der Feldkommandant,

gez. KNACKFUSS,

Oberst.

St, Helier, den 13. Januar 1942.

Fig. 3: **The well known photograph of the D 7 sign at the junction of Queen's Road and Undercliffe Road which was daubed with "V" slogans on 1 July, 1941. The Germans threatened reprisals if those responsible did not own up; nobody did own up and as a result all wireless sets were confiscated from houses in the neighbourhood and all males between the ages of 18 and 55 had to patrol the streets around Rouge Bouillon during the hours of darkness. Another white arrow from the 1940 system is visible at the foot of the wall. (C.I.O.S. (Jersey)).**
Fig. 4: **A further outbreak of traffic sign daubing took place in January, 1942.**

If this was, as the name implied, meant to be an island ring road, then the *Inselring* had some curious omissions in that it ignored such important points as Plemont, La Corbière and St. Brelade's Bay.

The new diversionary routes, or *Querstrassen*, were as follows:-

Qu "yellow" – proceeded from La Rocque Harbour through the country parishes by precisely the same route as the erstwhile Qu 1 until it reached St. Peter's Church; thence it went to Le Port (centre of St. Ouen's Bay) via Mont du Jubilé instead of proceeding to Red Houses via Route des Quennevais.

Qu "green" – left St. Helier via Elizabeth Place, Rouge Bouillon, Queen's Road, and Sion to Hérupe where it linked up with Qu "yellow" which it followed precisely to the foot of Mont des Routeurs from whence it proceeded down St. Peter's Valley, then Mont du Presbytere, Route du Manoir, Grande Route de St. Pierre, Rue des Landes, Route du Coin, Rue des Mans, and the southern part of Petite Route des Mielles that used to be known as Tabor Lane, terminating at Route des Genets.

The peculiar feature about Qu "green" was that, although it paralleled Qu "yellow" from Hérupe to St. Peter's Valley, it totalled ignored the one-way system of the latter route and was two-way over its entire length.

Important junctions on all roads were still marked with large signboards by Le Brocq and Borney but at all other junctions the signposts were provided by the military authorities. For the "red roads", these consisted of white boards about four feet long and twelve inches high which were edged in red and bore a double or single ended arrow, also in red, as well as the appropriate road number in white centred in a red circle. (See Fig.4). The *Inselring* signs were identical, but painted blue instead of red and displaying a blue R.

Signs for the Qu roads were shorter and pointed at one, or both ends. They were not edged in colour but the appropriate colour was applied to the arrow, the head of which also displayed, in red, the number of the adjacent "red road" to which the arrow pointed. (See also Fig.4). The wooden signposts produced by the military, as opposed to the Le Brocq and Borny examples, were of a shoddy standard, the paintwork being very "wishy-washy" in appearance.

With the passage of some 47 years since the end of World War II it might be thought that all traces of the German road number signs would have disappeared. This is certainly almost true of the wooden signboards for most of these were snapped up for firewood immediately after the Liberation in 1945; thus it is extremely fortunate that three surviving examples for "red 7" (one double-ended and two single-ended) have been presented to the C.I.O.S. in Jersey and these may be seen on display in the Command Bunker at Noirmont Point.

Fig. 5: A cluster of road signs captured by an official German photographer in the autumn of 1944 near La Hougue Bie on the St. Saviour/Grouville parish border. The lower sign on "red 3" points to Faldouet and the Qu sign with the 2 at the tip points to Le Catillon and "red 2" at Grouville Church. Breslau was the Casualty Receiving Station (Truppenverbandsplatz) located at "Grouville Court" almost opposite Grouville Parish Church. (C.I.O.S. (Jersey)).

Fig. 6: Despite being 52 years old when this photograph was taken in January, 1992, the arrow, surmounted by 1,2 and painted in 1940, is still discernible on the wall just to the west of Longueville Manor Hotel, St. Saviour.

Of the Qu road signs, two wall painted examples lingered on until about ten years ago, one at the foot of Le Catillon, Grouville, and the other at Hérupe, St. John, but time has taken its toll. Most other wall painted arrows have disappeared, not only because of the ravages of time, but as a result of road widening schemes and cars careering out of control which have both combined to destroy the walls on which the signs were painted.

By a strange quirk of fate, the best surviving examples are those of the 1940/41 era of painted arrows and numbers which directed traffic to specific defensive positions and these are all on the main road to Grouville, via Longueville and Grouville Hill. On the wall of Longueville Manor Hotel is a faint arrow surmounted by the figures 1, 2 (see Fig.6); a somewhat fragmented example occurs a few yards further on, while a third, similar arrow is tucked away behind an electricity sub-station on the nearby junction with Rue St. Thomas.

Opposite Grouville Parish Hall, on the wall of the house known as "Noirmont", and once again next to an electricity sub-station is another 1,2 albeit somewhat faded. Until quite recently the gateposts of La Croix Cemetery at Grouville were flanked by two more arrows, one displaying 1 and the other 2. The latter finally faded away about 1991 and the former fell victim to an errant car in 1988.

A similar fate befell a good example of D 10 on the gatepost of "Cherry Cottage" at the southern end of St. Peter's Valley in the late 1970s, but the best surviving sign of all, a very prominent D8, 11, 12, 13, 14 at the junction of Victoria Avenue/St. Aubin's Road; St. Peter's Valley at Bel Royal, was physically removed with scrapers and wire brushes in the 1960s!

For the reason why, we have to go back to the beginning of this article . . . hire cars! It was discovered that the numerous traffic hold-ups that were occuring at the western end of Victoria Avenue were caused by the drivers of hire cars, newly arrived in the island and on their first expedition to St. Breelaide's or St. Owen's Bay (sic), who would come face to face with this redundant but still obvious German traffic sign and stop dead to scan their maps to see if the signs would lead them to their destination!

For assistance readily given in the compilation of this article, we are grateful to Robin Cox, for information supplied, and to Alan Allix and Martin Walton for allowing us to examine the official German wartime maps of the road numbering systems which they have in their personal collections.

Part II of this article, dealing with Guernsey, will appear in the next edition of the *C.I. Occupation Review.*

DEPORTATION FROM GUERNSEY 1942 – TWO PERSONAL ACCOUNTS AND A GERMAN ASSESSMENT

Ken Tough

In the Autumn of 1941 the British government declared its intention to intern several hundred civilian German specialists working in Iran, who it considered posed a security threat to the vital supply route through that country to the embattled Soviet Union. Hitler's response was to threaten to deport ten 'selected Englishmen' from the Channel Islands to camps in eastern Poland for every German to be interned in Iran. In the event some 500 Germans were so interned; the German Foreign Ministry and the Wehrmacht between them were therefore given the task of selecting and deporting some 5,000 'Englishmen'. The Island authorities were directed to provide estimates of the number of residents born in the United Kingdom, and this produced a grand total of 8,166 for the Islands as a whole. It was soon clear that the 10 to 1 ratio could not be achieved if the selection were to be on a 'like for like' basis, given that the British had limited internment to men of military age; the German Feldkommandantur estimated that after allowing for essential workers and the sick no more than 1,200 would be available. The project appeared fraught with diplomatic and logistical difficulties and was quietly shelved until, almost a year later, a well-intentioned enquiry by the Swiss government – in its role as Protecting Power – drew Hitler's attention to the fact that his reprisal edict had been ignored.

This time there was to be no prevarication. On 15th September, 1942, the Island authorities were abruptly informed that all British subjects who were not normally resident in the Islands – for instance those caught there by the Occupation – and all men between 16 and 70 years of age not born in the Islands 'who belong to the English people' together with their families, were to be evacuated to Germany forthwith. The shock of the deportation was all the greater because of the speed with which it was carried out; in Jersey most deportees initially had less than 12 hours to organise their affairs; within two weeks the process was complete, with 1,186 persons deported from Jersey and 825 from Guernsey. A second, smaller deportation occurred in February, 1943, involving 115 men and 86 women and children. In an obvious change of policy the Germans allowed no newspaper publicity on this occasion, although rumours of impending action were rife in both Islands; in Guernsey it became known that FK515 officers had been searching in the identity card files held at the Greffe and at the end of December, 1943, the Controlling Committee was told by the

Germans to supply details of everyone convicted of criminal offences during the previous 10 years. The categories chosen for deportation included Jews and high-ranking Freemasons, former officers and reserve officers in the Armed Forces of the Crown, 'social undesirables' – as defined by the German occupiers – and several families of Sarkees removed from their homes as part of the German response to the British commando raid on Sark on 3rd/4th October, 1942.

To mark the 50th anniversary of the deportations the Channel Islands Occupation Society (Guernsey) held three well-attended meetings, the first a reunion on 26th September, 1992, to which all surviving ex-deportees were invited, followed by two meetings at which individual ex-deportees recounted their experiences. Subsequently ex-deportees have campaigned at the highest level in the United Kingdom and Germany for compensation from the German government for their illegal treatment, so far without success.

The following accounts throw new light on the deportation crisis and the way that indidivual lives were thrown into turmoil.

A couple who were deported . . . .

Eric and Ruth Sirett had been married for just twelve weeks when they were deported in September, 1942, on the ground of Eric's English birth. Eric, who had studied at commercial art school, first came to Guernsey on holiday in 1939. He took a job at the Guernsey Press Co. in the bookbinding department, with expectations of becoming a litho engraver/printer when the company expanded into litho work. That development was frustrated by the outbreak of war and then the Occupation, and Eric worked on a variety of tasks with the Press, including the gumming of the pioneer issues of Guernsey postage stamps. His skills in graphic design were put to good use in the production of posters and other artwork at Biberach internment camp. After liberation he worked for The Star newspaper as a process engraver and photographer before setting up in business as a commercial photographer. Eric has kindly provided the following personal account recording his experience of deportation half a century ago.

The Channel Islands had already been occupied by Nazi Germany for over two years when, without any warning, a notice appeared in the *Guernsey Evening Press* on 16th September, 1942, ordering all persons of English birth to be prepared for "evacuation" to Germany; a printed form had to be filled in and returned to the Greffe before noon on 18th September. When this bombshell burst, Ruth and I had been married for just three months and in fact, after the initial shock had worn off a bit, we joked to friends that Hitler was inviting us to the Continent for a delayed honeymoon.

Arriving at the Guernsey Press Co. that morning, I found that five other employees were also involved. As the Press was providing an essential service they had however been granted exemption for two employees; one oldish man had been born in England but returned to Guernsey as a baby, so he was first choice, and another who operated the Monotype machine was also exempted.

On 18th September we received our deportation orders to report to the Gaumont Cinema at noon on 21st September, and there was a list of things that we must take including some provisions, a blanket and, if possible, 10 Reichsmarks for each person. There was very little time to prepare for the journey and settle our affairs; Ruth and I were renting a small house at Delancey and our friend Bill Green kindly arranged to collect all our furniture and store it in a room above his shop.

This was a great help, and we were able to concentrate on acquiring the essential things we needed. One of the most useful items was an aluminium camping dixie, four dishes with handles that fitted one inside another into one compact unit. We both cooked with it for nearly three years and still have it among our souvenirs. Like many other people we also took the tools of our trades; Ruth packed hairdressing scissors, clippers and even small curling tongs, while I managed to stow away a small box of watercolours, brushes, pencils and two sketch pads. Two men in our contingent actually carried a small sewing machine each which were worth their weight in gold; one used his to produce battle-dress style suits out of grey German blankets.

The next two days were quite harrowing. Ruth and I were 22 and 23 years old respectively and we found it bad enough, but older people with children must have found it terrifying, especially not knowing what the Germans' intentions were. Some families were in distress because of the shortages of shoes and clothing which were rationed, but the States Controlling Committee and many Island charities responded to their needs immediately.

Zero day finally arrived, and we duly reported to the Gaumont Cinema, loaded with as much as we could carry, where we spent most of the morning sitting in the stalls waiting for things to happen. Dr Rose and Dr Sutcliffe kept hurrying in and out, desperately arguing with the Germans as they tried to obtain last minute exemptions for elderly people on medical grounds. At last everybody was accounted for and we were all issued with a wooden tomato box containing rations for the journey, including soap, shaving soap and tobacco. Some items such as chocolate, sardines and liver pâté had been taken from secret emergency stocks and were most welcome.

About 450 people made up this first contingent and we were taken in buses down to the harbour where Frank Stroobant and M. and Mdme. C. Pommier had prepared a meal of hot lamb stew using two borrowed

German field kitchens. We also received some ham sandwiches and a hardboiled egg each, courtesy of Frank Stroobant who himself was due to be deported with the second batch.

A nasty shock was in store when we began boarding the two transports however, because although the S.S. *La France* was a small passenger ship, the M.V. *Robert Müller 8* was a cargo boat that had only a small saloon and a large hold that had obviously been used recently for shipping live cattle. There were about twelve long wooden forms standing on the floor which would surely be thrown about in the prevailing rough seas. One toilet and washroom was available near the saloon but the main lavatories were two steel half-open structures, bolted onto the foredeck one each side of the bows. There was a gale forecast, which meant that anyone desperate enough to use one of these loos would be soaked by waves breaking over the bows. This vessel was completely unsuitable for women and children and a States deputation asked the Germans to postpone the sailing until a more suitable ship was obtained. Even the ship's captain supported them, and eventually the Kommandant agreed to abandon the sailing until morning when the weather might have improved.

We spent a very uncomfortable night on the floor of the hold, but by morning conditions at sea were worse and it was decided to send everyone back ashore leaving our belongings on board. Going home to await further instructions was impossible for some people because they had cleared their homes of furniture and many of these were accommodated at the Town Hospital. Ruth and I stayed with her mother in St. Peter Port.

The next morning we walked down to the harbour to look at the sea. At the Weighbridge we met Louis Guillemette, who was then Secretary to the President of the Controlling Committee. Ruth knew him and he asked us if we would accompany him onto the two ships to see if any of the perishable food in the baskets had gone bad. Showing the guard his port permit, he took us first to the *Robert Müller 8* where all our things were as we had left them, but quite a number of people had left some of the ham sandwiches which were now smelling a bit ripe. These we threw to the hungry seagulls together with some rotten grapes, before moving on to the *La France* and continuing the operation. There were some French dock workers on the Jetty and they asked us for the sandwiches that we had started to throw away. Louis obliged them, and after removing the smelly ham, they wolfed down the bread almost as voraciously as the gulls. The Germans had conscripted the poor devils as labourers and then kept them half starved and treated almost like slaves.

There was still no sign of another ship, but when we left Louis at the Pollet he assured us that negotiations were continuing in an attempt to replace the *Robert Müller 8*.

Eric and Ruth Sirett – A photograph taken in England in June 1945, a few days after their return from Biberach. (Eric Sirett).

I was very concerned about the insanitary conditions however, and the following day walked into Le Riche's Stores in the High Street and asked to see the manager with a view to obtaining some sort of disinfectant. He was most sympathetic and to my surprise supplied me with a litre bottle full of Jeyes' Fluid, now unobtainable in the shops, explaining that they were keeping the last drum for emergencies such as this. He then asked if there was anything I needed for ourselves, but I could only think how useful a tin of condensed milk would be, knowing that this had also disappeared long since. He walked across the office and swung open the door of a large metal safe, revealing about two dozen tins of Nestles, and, grinning at my astonishment, presented me with two small tins. Thanking him, I left with my trophies. I was proved right regarding their usefulness because the Germans only supplied fresh milk for the children and we made our tins last for over two weeks. As it happened, the disinfectant was not needed after all for when we finally left Guernsey two days later the *Robert Müller 8* had been replaced by another passenger ship, the S.S. *Minotaure.*

By then we were almost glad to get away because there had been another false alarm on Thursday, 24th September, and our farewells were becoming almost farcical. The ships sailed after midnight and joined a small convoy, but the sea was still very choppy and it rained all night . . . I laid six kapok lifejackets on the deck under one wing of the bridge, which gave us some shelter, although water did run under the lifejackets while we lay on them huddled under a large blanket, and the young ship's wireless operator kept stepping over us to get in or out of the radio room.

We docked at St. Malo at 7.00 a.m. and everybody received half of a rye loaf and a link of bacon sausage before boarding the train. Shortly after leaving we were also issued with a slab of chocolate each, a gift from the States of Guernsey which had been in the care of the St. John Ambulance men. Everyone thought things were looking up, but it was all that we were to receive for the whole three day journey, during which the toilets ran out of water and my bottle of Jeyes' Fluid came into its own.

I have already written an account of the next three years of internment, which I hope will be published in the near future, but I will briefly relate here a few incidents that are worthy of record.

The first was witnessing the terrible destruction that had been meted out to the city of Cologne in retaliation for the huge German raid on Coventry. On the third evening of our journey we had reached Cologne and as the train slowly passed over bridges we could see street after street blocked with the rubble of collapsed buildings; houses beside the railway line were just empty, smoke-blackened shells. How people could still inhabit the city was hard to believe, but when our train stopped at one of the platforms crowds of civilians were waiting there for transport out to the suburbs. Darkness fell and the train was blacked out, but we could see flashes from bombs falling further up the line and a rumour spread that we were to remain there for the night, fortunately groundless, because after another hour our journey was resumed and we reached Dorsten camp unscathed.

Over a year later, in Biberach, we actually saw American Flying Fortress bombers assembling before a raid on either Stuttgart or Munich. It was a beautiful sunny morning when people out on the main compound saw a flight of perhaps twenty four planes approaching from the west at a great height. Other flights began to appear on either side and I suddenly noticed that they were also flying across as far as the eye could see to the north and south, while around the overhead flights tiny flashes of reflected sunlight picked out the fighter escorts. Vapour trails were forming and from these we realised that many of the flights were circling and that we were in the centre of a vast assembly area. By now practically everybody was outside gazing upwards. Some people, who had begun counting the first planes, eventually gave up when the numbers reached over one thousand, especially as the increased thunder of engines denoted more flights coming in at lower altitudes.

Strips of silver paper a foot long by an inch wide started drifting down on the camp in their hundreds, and, at first, the children were warned not to pick them up, but someone who worked outside explained that it was harmless and being dropped to interfere with the German radar. Soon the whole sky overhead was crisis-crossed with vapour trails and many planes must already have reached their target because from a distance came the heavy rumble of explosions.

I suddenly noticed that one bomber had started to descend from its group and smoke was blowing back from the fuselage. It began a slow circle over the camp and Biberach town, dropping seven parachutists at intervals until finally it disappeared into the valley. There was no explosion and later we heard that it had been put onto automatic pilot while the crew baled out, and it had actually landed, with the fire out, almost intact. Some of our men out on a wood fatigue a day later passed close to the plane and their guard stopped to allow them to inspect it, as much for his curiosity as anything. Strangely, it was completely unguarded and just as it had been when the crew evacuated, with machineguns at the firing points and belts of ammunition lying around. Our men were awestruck by the sheer size of it and there was much speculation as to the huge amount of bombs it could carry.

As Ruth and I grow older we realise more fully how difficult it must have been for the more elderly internees to adjust to this existence, the lack of privacy for instance being a source of much embarrassment, especially for very shy ladies. Lack of decent food was also harder on people who had been used to a fairly high standard, although the two years of occupation must already have prepared them to some extent. To the younger generation though it taught self-reliance and adaptability, especially in the first few months at Biberach with temperatures often below zero. It is impossible to describe the misery caused by a combination of intense cold and malnutrition; it has to be experienced.

Some idea might be gauged by a one-off issue of dried fish at a time when we were almost starving. The fillets, possibly of haddock, appeared to have been sun dried and fly blown during the process, because every piece contained dried maggots. Nearly everybody just scraped off the worst parts and ate the rest. Ruth and I mashed up ours with my ration of two small potatoes and baked it in the ash pan of our large stove during the short period that it was alight. It tasted delicious. Regular issues of Red Cross parcels gradually eased the food situation however, until eventually some internees hardly ever drank the soup, and men used the hot bramble leaf tea for shaving with.

Life was not all gloom and doom. Many people were talented entertainers, and every week there was either a play or a variety show taking place in the theatre hut with our camp orchestra valiantly coping with all the demands upon their resources. Some of the musicians also doubled up as a very popular dance band, playing for both modern and old time dances, but I do not think people realised how hard they worked and the difficulties they experienced while trying to rehearse in the unheated hut in sub-zero temperatures.

Biberach itself is in a very beautiful area of southern Germany, two thousand feet above sea level near the edge of the Black Forest. One of my most lasting memories is of walking out of my barrack and seeing a great range of snow covered mountains towering up in a semi-circle to the east and south of the camp. Freak weather conditions were giving us an awe-inspiring view of the Austrian and Swiss Alps, some of which must have been over a hundred miles away. This magnificent spectacle remained for most of the day before gradually disappearing, and we never set eyes on it again!

There is so much to remember of this period, some good, some bad and some extremely funny, but all things considered most people coped very well and many revealed unexpected talents which they used for the benefit of others.

. . . and a couple who were spared

The Reverend R. Douglas Ord was a Methodist minister in the English circuit in Guernsey, based at Brock Road Church, from 1938 to 1948. His manse was at 'Shelton', Rohais, St Peter Port. Throughout the Occupation he kept a diary which ran to some 1,050 typewritten pages and which was deposited at the Priaulx Library in 1992. Ord had learnt German as a prisoner of war in Germany during the First World War. He declined to act as an official interpreter during the Occupation, fearing this would compromise his independence. His diary records contacts with military chaplains and other German personnel, some of whom spoke freely to Ord of their disillusionment with the Nazi regime. The following extracts, reproduced by kind permission of Dr Harry Tomlinson, chief librarian at the Priaulx Library, describe Ord's initial dismay at impending deportation in September, 1942, and his subsequent exemption.

"G." is Ord's wife Hilda Graham Ord, known as "Grae". "Mr Blampied" is Charles Bertram Blampied of La Fosse, St Martin's, father of the late Jurat Guy Blampied. Heinrich Bödeker was a minister in the German Evangelical Church who had been identified as politically unsound by the authorities and conscripted into the Kriegsmarine; both he and his friend Reinhold Zachmann were serving in a coastal artillery battery in Guernsey. They became friendly with Ord, keeping him informed on what was actually happening in Germany and also calling at the manse to listen to German broadcasts by the B.B.C.

September 15th

An evil day for Guernsey

I was doing my best to prune the fruit bushes in the garden, feeling very tired and unlike effort, when I became aware of G. coming down the path with a grave face. Someone had just rung up to ask if I knew anything about the Order for the Deportation of the English-born people. We had heard nothing. It seemed just another of the rumours of which we had had so many. Twelve months ago we were distressed about the threats in connection with the alleged Iran atrocities. Of course, *a priori*, there was nothing to lead us to disbelieve a suggestion that these people who held us now would act in such a way. Yet it seemed best to await something definite. Half an hour later my neighbour handed me the *Evening Press* and said: "Here it is at last!" The now notorious Knackfuss had one more of his *Bekanntmachungen* as follows:-

"By order of higher authorities the following British subjects will be evacuated and transferred to Germany. (a) Persons who have their permanent residence not on the Channel Islands; for instance, those who have been caught here by the outbreak of war; (b) All those men not born on the Channel Islands and 16 to 70 years of age who belong to the English people, together with their families. Detailed instructions will be given by the Feldkommandantur 515.

Der Feldkommandant,
Knackfuss, Oberst".

Mr. and Mrs. Ord as photographed for their identity card at Candie Gardens on 1 August, 1941. He wrote in his diary: "After waiting in a queue some twenty minutes, we were told to put our heads in a sort of pillory and weren't even asked to smile. All over in a second. Then clerks checked up particulars afresh." They attended at St. Stephen's schoolroom on 9 October, 1941 for the photograph to be attached to their identity cards. Ord was not impressed with the portraiture. "We both look somewhat the worse for wear in these pictures." (The Greffe).

This was a dreadful blow and left one stunned. Germany! A prison camp! And for the second time in my life. And to have to bear the thought of G. going through what I knew so well – the journey, the food question, the conditions of camp life, the plundering of our home and goods, and the ending of my work so dear to me. Yet the implications of the Order were so vast that it seemed inevitable that modifications must follow. The Island life would be paralysed if all the English-born were deported. Two doctors only would remain. All the dentists are English. Banks would be robbed of the major part of their staffs. Persons holding vital and probably irreplaceable posts of a technical character would be taken. Churches no doubt would receive scant consideration from the Nazis. Two of the five on the staff of the Methodist Church were Channel Islanders. The others would be involved. Though we have had some shocks these years, nothing like this had come our way as yet. And now that the blow has fallen rumour begins to add to the wretchedness. It is being said that the cause is the destruction of German cities and that those deported would be quartered in the raided or to-be-raided areas. On the principle of "Bomb us and you bomb your own as well!" But without conjuring up imaginative situations there is enough to give cause for anxiety. The winter will be upon us. We cannot hope to be allowed much luggage. We have just passed through a terribly trying winter which has reduced the stamina and resistance of our people. But one thing is sure: we shall be behind barbed wire! For supper we plunged on one of our jealously-guarded tins of salmon.

Amid this new distress it is easy to overlook other matters among which is a Notice stating that a German Court Martial has recently imprisoned and heavily fined a Barter dealer for "selling articles in daily use at excessive prices in France". Knackfuss has another Order forbidding civilians to carry or pass on any kind of mail or information whilst travelling between the Islands and the Continent. To sweeten these Orders we are told that we may have a ration of 100 saccharines.

September 16th

From breakfast onwards the telephone rang without intermission while people continually called to express sympathy or to offer help. Disregarding the danger of being tapped, Mr Blampied rang up to ask "What do you think of this filthy German Order?" This well-known Islander said that unless modifications could be arranged all the key-men would be taken away. The milkman's comment was: "They ought to take the lot of us to make it fair!" – a generous thought on the part of a Guernsey-born. I had a meeting in the afternoon where nearly everyone was outside the scope of the Order. Their concern and sympathy were overwhelming. On my return I met G. in Town. She told me the place was full of the wildest rumours. Advocate Sherwill was reported as having said that four hundred had already left Jersey, though the Order had only appeared the previous night. As yet we have no confirmation of this. Later it was said that there would be a very wide margin between those liable and those taken. People in important positions will not, it is believed, have to go. Churches will hardly come into that category in Nazi eyes. The Island Authorities have put a number of questions to the Kommandantur and these will require time to answer. Rumour has it that two expert fishermen have got away in a 25ft boat for England. Some say they have been drowned. Others that they had several hours' start and ought to get through. If they do what steps will the British Government take?

September 17th

At breakfast time Reinhold came to offer his sympathy and indignation. He spoke with scorn of the pledge that we should be respected. Other people began calling in distress asking for advice as people did at the beginning of the pre-Occupation evacuation. By noon tomorrow we have to send in particulars of households to the Greffier.

[. . . . .]

So much of the distress is due to the Germans who characteristically have bungled the whole arrangements. Had they explained why the deportation was being carrried out and what would be the conditions, much anxiety would have been avoided. But nothing was said about conditions of travel or of internment, nor were any instructions given about packing what was needed or would be permitted. The Order was baldly flung down by Knackfuss without word of explanation. It is not clear whether this was of set purpose or just clumsiness. The effect is the same, however.

September 18th

I confess I did not sleep all night. Memories of the imprisonment in 1918 and of the dreadful train journey to Germany haunted me, tired out though I was and feeling very far from well. The shock, together with the thought that G. would now face what I had once been through, weighed me down. And now this morning the rain is coming in sheets and all seemed black. There was so much to do and there came so many people to see us or to ask advice that we hardly knew where we stood. At breakfast Bödeker turned up in a state of great sympathetic distress to offer us not only sympathy, but money should it be required. We told him we were to be allowed only ten marks each. "In Germany," he said, "that is really more than you will need, for there is nothing you could buy." He offered to write to his people and to Dr Wilhelm Vischer of Basel as soon as he could get our internment camp address. Vischer, he thought, might send German books and other things. "After this Nazi regime has been destroyed there will be revolution in my country. If you are not repatriated immediately and you can get out of the camp, make your way to my home where my father will shelter you till he can see you safely out of Germany. He will be glad to do something towards repaying your kindness to me." As he left his feelings got the better of him for his is a most sensitive nature. "Do you remember what you said to me when I was in such trouble some time ago?" he asked. "You quoted Psalm XLVI.2 Luther's version:

"Gott ist unsere Zuversicht und Stärke,
Eine Hilfe in der grössen Nöten
Die uns getroffen haben."
This I now say to you!"

[. . . . .]

September 19th
[. . . . .]

Our name was now before Dr Brosch and placed on the list of deportees. But at this last moment the unexpected happened. The 'phone rang and I took the call. It was from the Guernsey-born Superintendent of the French circuit who had been the go-between at the Feldkommandantur. He spoke five words: "You are not to go!" I could only just get voice enough to ask for an explanation, which came as follows. A Minister from Jersey, Donald Stuart had decided to retire from the active work [. . . . .] He had property in Guernsey and resolved to come here and live on it. Arrived at the White Rock, St. Peter Port, the Germans looked at his passport and said: "You are English: you go to Germany." Now, continued Mr Beaugié, it was pointed out to Dr Brosch that they had got three Ministers as required by them – two had volunteered and here was a third but the passport people were sending him as an ordinary civilian. Why, if go he must, should he not go as a padre? Dr Brosch, probably wearied by the whole affair, assented and struck out my name and entered that of Stuart. The matter was therefore absolutely decided. Hardly able to credit this good fortune I cross-questioned Beaugié who categorically affirmed that he had *seen* Dr Brosch strike out my name and write in that of Stuart. So we were cut down at the eleventh hour. I hung up the receiver and went into the study where there was little but the empty shelves and desk and table and chairs. I sat down feeling ill, and no wonder after the loss of weight earlier in the year through lack of food. G. came in and said: "Who was that you were talking to?" I told her the good news, and she disappeared, coming back with a little tot of brandy which, little as I like it, did me good.

[. . . . .]

While G. was in Town for the rations, she could hardly make her way through the streets for being stopped by people who wanted to know if we had to go or who had heard we had been exempted and wanted to say "thank God you are to stay". It is overwhelming, after all this time, to find that we have some place in the hearts of this community. It is thought probable that the destination of the evacuees is the Black Forest region. All notices are to be out by Sunday evening. Those who receive none are exempt. This is final. Went to bed as early as we might, dead tired, and slept.

The Deportations – A German Assessment

The following extracts from the monthly reports for September, 1942, and January, 1943, by the intelligence officer (Ic) on the staff of the German LXXXIX Army Corps, based at Saint-Lo and responsible for the Channel Islands, to the headquarters of Seventh Army at Le Mans, show how the Germans perceived the reaction in the Islands both to the deportations and to the unfolding disaster on the eastern front, where the final surrender at Stalingrad took place on 2nd February, 1943.

(i) *2nd October, 1942*

It is not yet possible to arrive at a general view on the effect on civilian morale of the evacuation of more than 2,000 British citizens from the English Channel Islands. The action naturally alarmed the people of the Islands, although this would have been alleviated by the welfare measures taken by the Germans during the evacuation. The evacuees in general exhibited correct and self-assured composure, in keeping with the English character. Two elderly married couples, who were due to be evacuated, could not however reconcile themselves to separation from home and committed suicide.

(ii) *1st February, 1943*

The new preparations for evacuation aroused obvious concern amongst the people of the British Channel Islands. Confidence in the ultimate victory of the English motherland has grown as a result of recent developments in the war.

(iii) *3rd March, 1943*

The attitude of the population in the Channel Islands remains substantially the same. The newspapers published in English by the Germans are avidly read. The main concern of the people is the further evacuation which has become necessary.

OBITUARIES

Leslie Philip Sinel

Born in the year 1906, Leslie Philip Sinel began work with the *Evening Post* in 1920, at the age of 14, as an apprentice printer.

By 1940 he had risen to the position of Works Foreman and, as such, it was his responsibility to produce the daily "Here & There" column which contained small, "newsy" items of local interest. When the German Army entered Paris in June, 1940, Leslie Sinel conceived the idea of also maintaining a daily diary for the benefit of posterity as he realised that these were indeed momentous times.

When the Germans occupied Jersey he kept the diary going, at no small risk to himself as a colleague at the *"E.P."* received a stiff prison sentence on the mere *suspicion* of keeping a diary.

Leslie Sinel missed nothing! The *Occupation Diary*, as it became known (the correct title of the work when it was eventually published in 1945 was *The German Occupation of Jersey*), contained everything; the results of football matches, alterations to the ration scale, naval engagements, when the flak batteries opened up, theatrical productions, troop movements, the amount of the parish rate . . . everything! Although he did employ a few "agents" to gather information, most of the contents were his own work.

A high degree of accuracy was maintained and errors were few; this degree of accuracy was, in fact, remarkable, and can be checked now that many of the *Diary's* entries can be compared with the official War Diaries of the various German and British commands. (See, for example, the article "A Bridge over the Enemy" contained in the *C.I. Occupation Review 1984*).

One of the biggest compliments paid to Leslie Sinel came from the late Dr Charles Cruickshank, author of the official history of the Occupation, when he told me ". . . without Sinel's *Diary* I wouldn't have known where to start my researches".

Mr Sinel retired from the *Evening Post* in 1970 having risen to the position of Works Manager and director of the newspaper.

Retirement, however, did not mean idleness and he threw himself into his main interests which, amongst others, was his lifelong association with St. Helier's Parish Church. He also served on the St. Helier Welfare Board, the Church of England finance committee and with several other charitable organisations; he often gave talks on local history and wrote articles for various publications.

He will be well remembered for his generous and kindly nature and for his meticulous attention to detail in every respect; this included his dress and his former colleagues at the *"E.P."* recall how, in even the warmest of weather, Mr. Sinel would appear in the machine room dressed as always in waistcoat and collar and tie!

He was a devout Christian who really practised what he preached and although he was one of the first members of the Occupation Society, he would never attend the Society's early meetings because they were held in a room over a pub!

A great character who is sadly missed, Leslie Sinel passed away on 6 October, 1991 at the age of 85; the Occupation Society extends its sympathy to his widow and family.

Gordon Augustin Prigent

Born on 5 November, 1924, Gordon Prigent had the rare "distinction" of being one of the very few Channel Islanders who were imprisoned in the *SS* concentration camp *Lager Nordeney* in Alderney.

Having left school at the age of 15, Gordon was learning his trade as a builder and, as such, was called upon to carry out work of a non-military nature for the occupying forces as required under Article 53 of the Hague Convention. This led to a dispute with a German N.C.O. and Gordon, without stopping to think, kicked over a tin of paint and went home.

The next thing that he knew was that the *Feldgendarmerie* was on his doorstep; he was taken to the harbour and bundled off to Guernsey. A night in prison there, and the next move was to Alderney with a small number of other Channel Islanders in a similar predicament. On arrival, they were put to work on the *Organization Todt* farm, but once it was discovered that the men were British the group was given more congenial employment at the *Soldatenheim* where they acted as cleaners, gardeners, etc.

Whenever their "boss", a German *Sonderführer*, was out of the way, they would sneak into his office and listen to the B.B.C. All went well until the day that they were caught by one of the German Red Cross sisters who lost no time in reporting them. As a result, and to cut a long story short, they were collected by the *SS* and found themselves in the concentration camp where all manner of horrors had to be endured. Ill nourished and subject to beatings for no apparent reason, the men had to suffer hard physical labour which included quarrying, unloading ships, and concreting bunkers.

On the night of 5/6 June, 1944, Gordon and his immediate associates had to dig what they were told were fox holes, but which, he had no doubt, were in fact their own graves. No Allied landing on Alderney took place that night so they were spared, but a direct order from Hitler's H.Q. stipulated that on no account must the *SS* concentration

Leslie Philip Sinel 1906 - 1991. (W.M. Ginns).

Gordon Augustin Prigent 1924 - 1991. (Jersey Evening Post).

camp prisoners fall into Allied hands. The moment the Americans began advancing towards the Cherbourg peninsula all the prisoners were loaded onto a small cargo vessel which set sail for Cherbourg. By good fortune, they were too late as by now the Americans had cut across the bottom of the peninsula and all German forces thereon were cut off.

So it was back to Alderney for a few more weeks and then, with no prior warning, the prisoners were all loaded into the hold of a small coaster, standing packed tight as if on the London Underground during the rush hour. The hatches were battened down, the journey to Guernsey took ten hours and by this time many of the prisoners were on the point of suffocation, Gordon among them. Upon arrival, those who had collapsed were taken off to hospital where they remained for about one week while waiting for another ship to take them on to Jersey, and then St. Malo.

This delay was providential for Gordon, as by the time they reached Jersey, St. Malo was on the point of being besieged by the Americans and further communications were impossible. Gordon was thereupon freed and told to report to the German Harbour Police every day but, after a while, he didn't bother and, curiously for them, they lost interest in him. He joined the St. Helier Police as an auxiliary policeman and, as such, was on crowd control duty in the Royal Square on Liberation Day.

The years rolled by, but Gordon never spoke of his experiences in Alderney, until one day, with great reluctance on his part, he was persuaded to come to an Occupation Society meeting at which slides of Alderney's fortifications were to be shown. He sat through the meeting staring at the screen saying not a word, until a picture of Les Mouriaux water tower was projected, when he gave a sign of recognition. After the meeting he spoke briefly about his experiences, but later the same year he was again persuaded to come on a Society outing to Alderney. This was to be his first visit to the island for over 30 years.

I will remember how he stood in the middle of the remains of *Lager Nordeney* and, overcoming his emotion, began to recount his imprisonment. After that, he never looked back, and gave a long and interesting talk to the Occupation Society (which was recorded) and he was subsequently much in demand with TV producers when they were compiling documentaries about the Occupation. He was also a regular participant at the annual gatherings in Alderney of the French Association of Political Deportees.

Gordon devoted much of his time to the welfare of the late Walter Gallicham. The latter had also been in *Lager Nordeney* with Gordon and as a result of his bad treatment there, spent many years of his life in St. Saviour's Hospital. Gordon became a keen member of the Occupation Society and, in the early days of bunker preservation, was hand to carry out blocklaying and plastering. It is a safe bet that when he was labouring on the construction of bunkers in 1944, he would never have dreamt that the day would come when he would be helping to preserve them!

For many years Gordon was employed by the Jersey Electricity Company, but took early retirement and became busier than ever on various small building projects. Described by a former colleague as "one of the best", Gordon was also a member of the Caesarean Cycling Club, a keen table tennis player (he was still playing in his 60s!), and, above all, he loved his boat and the sea.

Gordon passed away on 1 November, 1991, while on holiday in Portugal. The Society extends its sympathy to his widow Iris, who joined the Society at the same time as her husband. He will be greatly missed.

W.M.G.

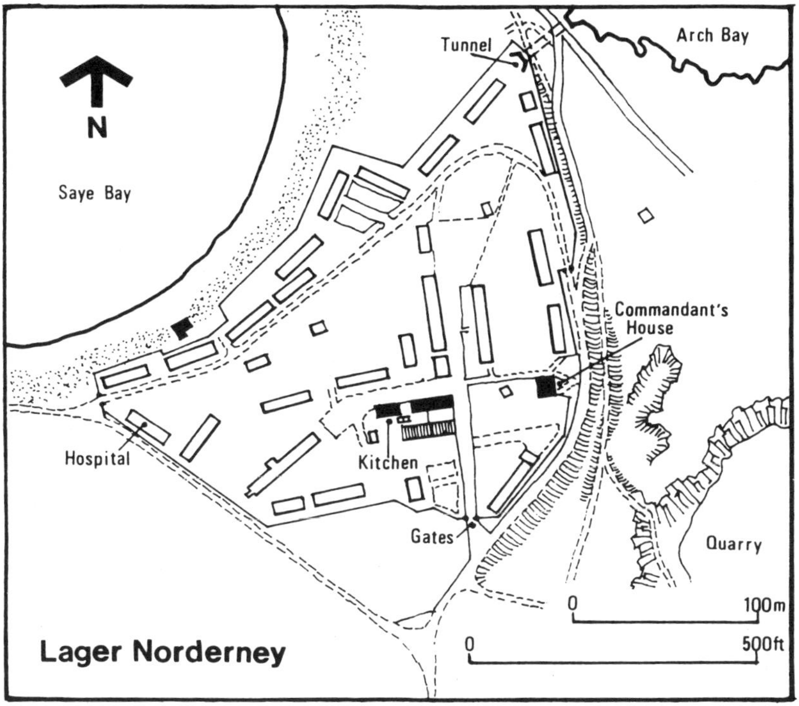

Plan of *Lager Norderney* published in *The Fortifications of Alderney* by Colin Partridge and Trevor Davenport. (128 pp, paperback, profusely illustrated with many scaled plans of the fortifications; £8.70 inc. postage from Alderney Publishers Ltd, 22 Victoria Street, Alderney)

JEWS DEPORTED FROM OCCUPIED GUERNSEY

Ken Tough

In Issue No. 18 of the *Channel Islands Occupation Review* Margaret Boden-Heaume summarised information about some 36 German and Austrian citizens, all women, who were reported as resident in Guernsey in March 1941. This was derived from a German file of letters exchanged with the Island authorities which found its way after the Liberation to the Yad Washem Museum in Jerusalem. It was known that three Jewish women had been deported by the Germans and it was assumed that they had been murdered, but no details were known. Since that article was published much more information has come to light, through the opening of the official Guernsey records on the Occupation, further research at the Yad Washem Museum and interviews with friends and relations of those who were deported.

It now appears that at the time the Occupation began in June 1940 there were at least five Jewish women of German or Austrian origin living in Guernsey; two, who had married Guernseymen, survived the Occupation; this present article describes what is known at present about the other three whose fate was, until recently, obscure. With the benefit of hindsight, it is surprising that all Jews did not leave for England to escape their potential Nazi persecutors. Some insight into this problem can be gained from examining public attitudes and Government policies in Great Britain and the Islands in the months preceding the Occupation.

In a series of lightning campaigns beginning on 9 April 1940 and culminating in the French armistice on 22 June, the Germans conquered first Denmark and Norway, and then the Low Countries and France. Many in Britain blamed these defeats, at least in part, on the clandestine activities of 'the enemy within,' the Fifth Column of German agents and their sympathisers. In addition to traitors within, the Germans had, it was widely believed, employed the novel weapon of parachute troops, often in disguise, to capture bridges and other key sites and generally subvert the defenders. Nor was fear of internal subversion verging on panic limited to the ill-informed man in the street; on returning to Britain on 14 May 1940, the senior British diplomat in Holland reported on the dire threat posed by enemy aliens: "Every German or Austrian servant, however superficially charming and devoted, is a real and grave menace . . ." and, when the signal was given, there would be agents ". . . all over the country who will at once embark on widespread sabotage and attacks on civilians and the military indiscriminately. We cannot afford to take this risk. ALL Germans and Austrians, at least, ought to be interned at once."

Although the ubiquitous Fifth Column and paratroopers in disguise were almost entirely imaginary, the *Grande Peur* which they engendered, and which German propaganda encouraged, was itself a potent weapon. It also had an immediate effect on Government policy towards enemy aliens in Britain. There were some 74,000 German or Austrian residents; of these more than 55,000 or 75 per cent had been recognised by the British authorities as refugees from Nazi oppression. However, in the three months up to the end of June 1940, more than 25,000 German and Austrian aliens, including many Jewish refugees, male and female, were interned and those still at large were subjected to a curfew and other restrictions. The strictest measures were taken in the areas of southern England considered most vulnerable to invasion from the Continent.

British Government policy in an area considered so vital to national security was naturally extended to the Channel Islands. The Home Office advised the Lieutenant-Governors to use their discretion in placing restrictions on enemy aliens. From 18 May onwards German aliens began to be interned in Guernsey; on 19 June eight German internees were shipped to Southampton; four days after the departure of the Lieutenant-Governor on 21 June his Secretary asked that all aliens should be released. Even more than in Britain, these measures in the Islands took place against a background of mounting confusion and panic as invasion loomed.

Until mid-June 1940, life in the Islands had continued virtually as normal; the shock was all the greater, therefore, when on 19 June – the very day that Rommel's tanks rolled into nearby Cherbourg – it was announced within the Islands – but not elsewhere – that all British forces were to be withdrawn and ships would be provided to evacuate, initially, schoolchildren, younger mothers and their children, and men of military age; this was extended within days to enable all who wished to seek refuge in the United Kingdom. Chaos ensued as individuals made up their minds whether to go or stay; in the event almost half the population of Guernsey left for England; in the general confusion many families were split up by the arrival of the Germans on 30 June.

Against this background it is not surprising that Thérèse Steiner, Auguste Spitz and Marianne Grunfeld, Jewish refugees from central Europe, under official surveillance and suspicion as enemy aliens and restricted in their movements, did not make good their escape to England. On the information presently available it is unclear whether they were prevented from leaving, or whether they had decided to stay in Guernsey, or whether, like so many Guernsey people, subject to official indecision and the ebb and flow of rumour, they were simply overwhelmed by events. However that may be, in retrospect it is plain that their fate was sealed by the German invasion.

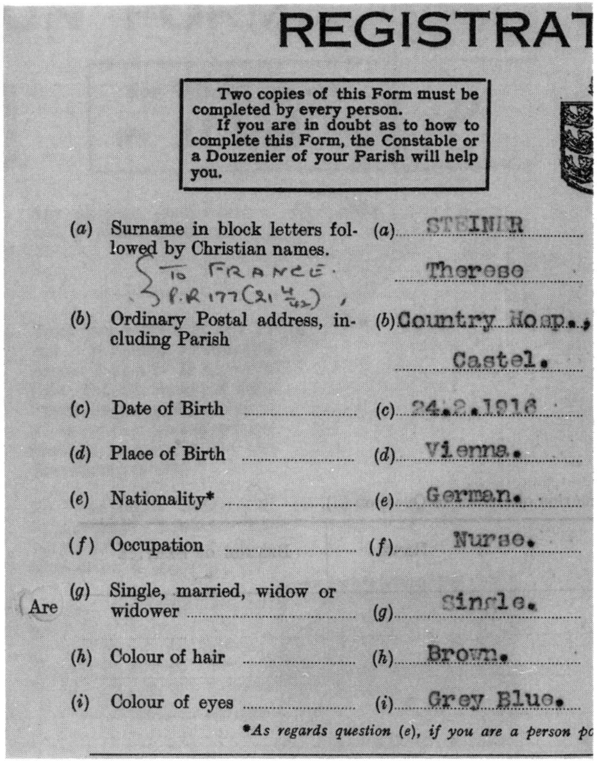

REGISTRAT

Two copies of this Form must be completed by every person.
If you are in doubt as to how to complete this Form, the Constable or a Douzenier of your Parish will help you.

(a)	Surname in block letters followed by Christian names. { To FRANCE. P.R 177 (21 4/42),	(a) STEINER Therese
(b)	Ordinary Postal address, including Parish	(b) Country Hosp., Castel.
(c)	Date of Birth	(c) 24.2.1916
(d)	Place of Birth	(d) Vienna.
(e)	Nationality*	(e) German.
(f)	Occupation	(f) Nurse.
Are (g)	Single, married, widow or widower	(g) Single.
(h)	Colour of hair	(h) Brown.
(i)	Colour of eyes	(i) Grey Blue.

*As regards question (e), if you are a person p

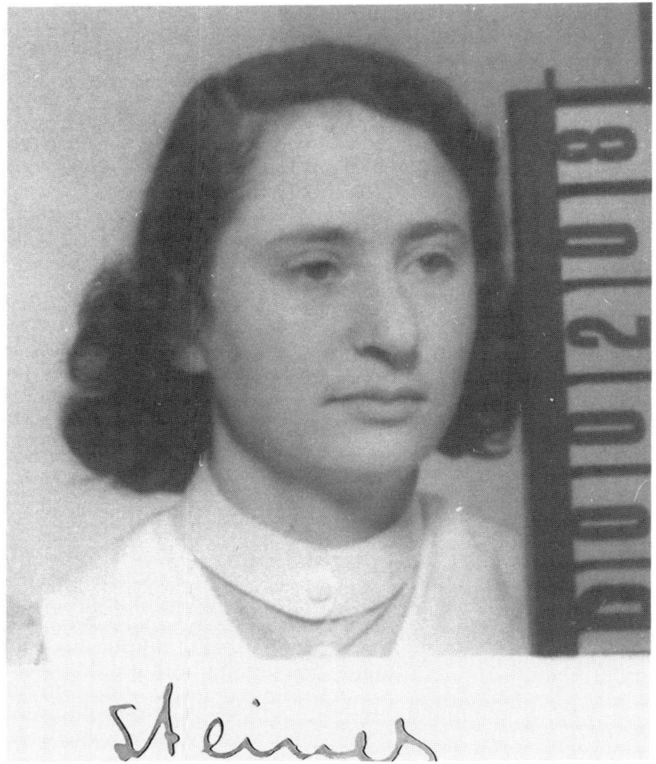

This and next two pages: Thérèse Steiner, "Auguste" Spitz and Marianne Grunfeld, as photographed for their identity cards in the summer of 1941, together with extracts from their registration forms. In each case the form is annotated "To France 21.4.42". (The Greffe).

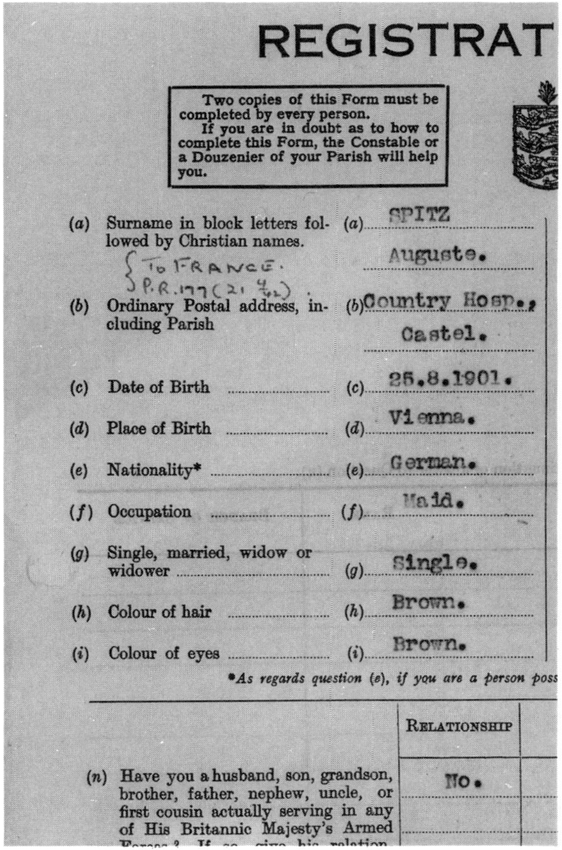

REGISTRAT

Two copies of this Form must be completed by every person.
If you are in doubt as to how to complete this Form, the Constable or a Douzenier of your Parish will help you.

(a)	Surname in block letters followed by Christian names. {To FRANCE. P.R.177 (21 4/42)	(a) SPITZ Auguste.
(b)	Ordinary Postal address, including Parish	(b) Country Hosp., Castel.
(c)	Date of Birth	(c) 25.8.1901.
(d)	Place of Birth	(d) Vienna.
(e)	Nationality*	(e) German.
(f)	Occupation	(f) Maid.
(g)	Single, married, widow or widower	(g) Single.
(h)	Colour of hair	(h) Brown.
(i)	Colour of eyes	(i) Brown.

*As regards question (e), if you are a person poss

	RELATIONSHIP
(n) Have you a husband, son, grandson, brother, father, nephew, uncle, or first cousin actually serving in any of His Britannic Majesty's Armed Forces? If so, give his relation	No.

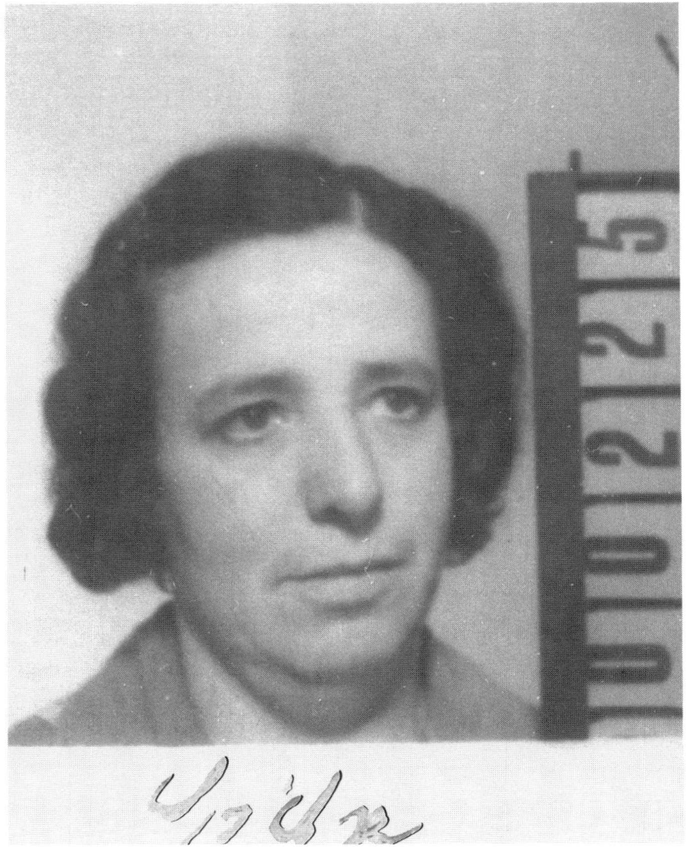

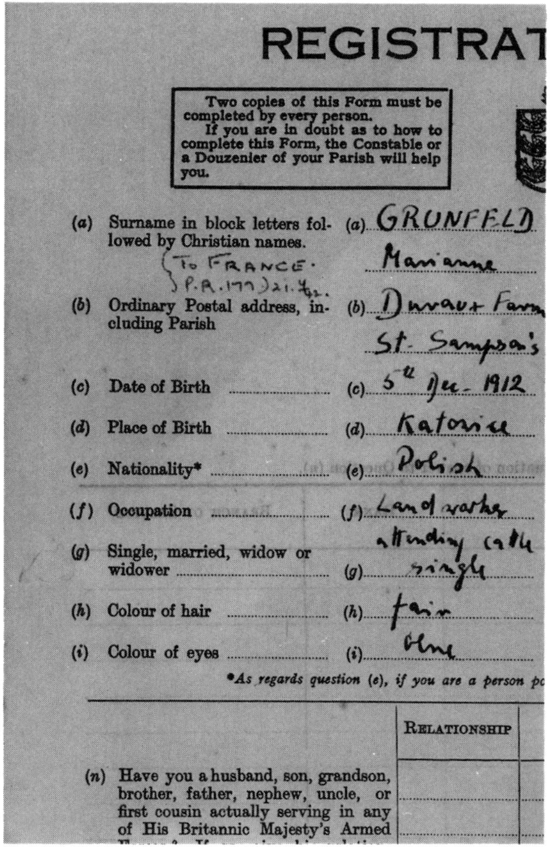

REGISTRAT

Two copies of this Form must be completed by every person.
If you are in doubt as to how to complete this Form, the Constable or a Douzenier of your Parish will help you.

(a) Surname in block letters followed by Christian names. (a) GRUNFELD Marianne
(To FRANCE. P.R.177) 21.4.42.

(b) Ordinary Postal address, including Parish (b) Duvaux Farm St. Sampson's

(c) Date of Birth (c) 5th Dec. 1912

(d) Place of Birth (d) Katowice

(e) Nationality* (e) Polish

(f) Occupation (f) Land worker attending cattle

(g) Single, married, widow or widower (g) single

(h) Colour of hair (h) fair

(i) Colour of eyes (i) blue

*As regards question (e), if you are a person p…

	Relationship
(n) Have you a husband, son, grandson, brother, father, nephew, uncle, or first cousin actually serving in any of His Britannic Majesty's Armed …	

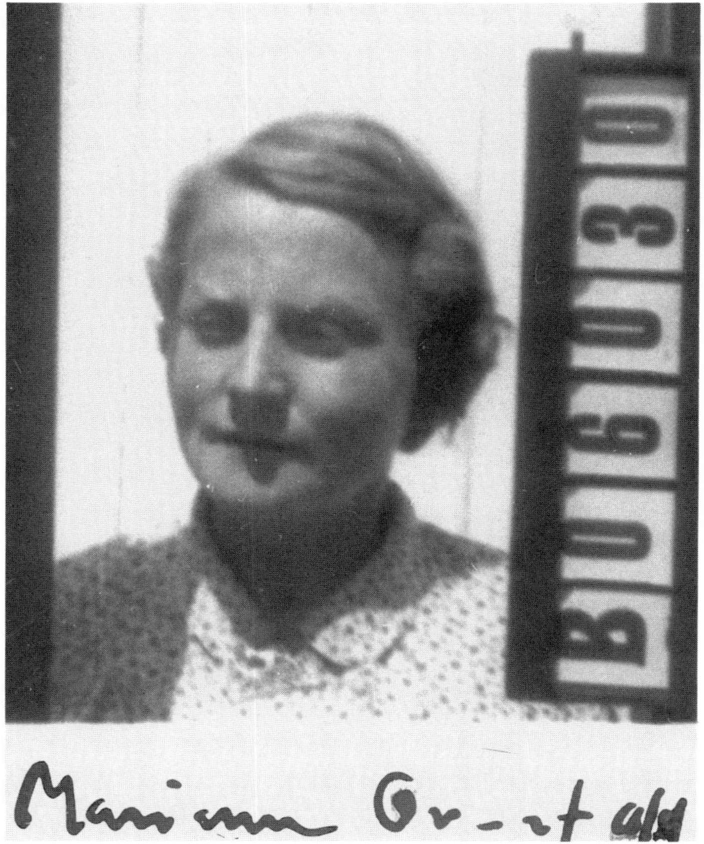

It is about Thérèse Steiner that most details have emerged to date. She was born in Vienna in February 1916; in 1937 she was sent by her family to the relative safety of England. She was engaged by Edgar Potts, a dentist of Beckenham in Kent, and his wife Marjory, as a nanny to look after their daughters, Wendy aged 7 and Angela aged 5. In 1939 the Potts family leased Rosebud Cottage in Sark – by coincidence the building in which the German surrender of that Island was signed on 10 May 1945 – as a holiday home. With his young family safely installed in Sark, Mr Potts returned to his practice in England. After six months in Sark Mrs Potts moved to Guernsey for the sake of her girls' education. Thérèse Steiner's career as a nanny was abruptly ended when she was interned as an enemy alien, first at Fort Richmond and later at the Emergency Hospital, which had been set up at the beginning of the war in the old Country Hospital buildings in the Castel. The Potts family left for England just before the Occupation.

The Germans naturally took an interest in German or Austrian nationals resident in the Islands. They required the civilian authorities to given details of aliens, including their date and place of birth, address, religion and nationality. Jewish refugees such as Therese Steiner found that whereas prior to the invasion they had been interned as enemy aliens because of their nationality, now they were in greater peril because of their Jewishness. Nazi anti-Semitic legislation began to be extended to the Islands as early as October 1940. The measures were relatively mild and gave no hint of the policy of outright extermination pursued from 1942 onwards. Jews in the Islands had to register with the authorities and later Jewish-owned businesses were either closed down or taken over.

For almost two years Thérèse Steiner was employed at the Emergency Hospital as a nurse and is remembered to this day as intelligent and well-liked; she played the piano and attended concerts at the Church of St James the Less in St Peter Port, now the St James Assembly and Concert Hall. Another Jewish refugee was employed at the Emergency Hospital at this time. Auguste Spitz, who also came from Vienna, was born on 25 August 1901 and worked in the hospital as a ward maid.

Marianne Grunfeld, the third of the trio of Jewish refugees, was a Polish Jew; she was born on 5 December 1912 at Kattowitz in the province of Silesia, which was assigned to Poland in 1921 following a plebiscite and renamed Katowice. Like her co-religionists she travelled to Britain and studied at Reading University from 1937 to 1939, where she gained a diploma in horticulture. Unable to return home to German-occupied Poland, she advertised for a farming job. In May 1940 she took up employment with Ted Ogier at Duveaux Farm, St Sampson's. She was urged by her employer to leave for England at the time of the evacuation; this was however a hectic period for the remaining farm-workers coping with the cattle which had been brought to Guernsey from Alderney after the human population of that Island had sailed *en masse* for England; events moved swiftly and by 30 June the last ship had left and Grunfeld, who had escaped the invasion of Poland the previous year, now in her turn faced the uncertainty of life under German occupation.

In a small Island community with few alien residents, and living cheek by jowl with a huge German garrison, it would have been impossible for these women, already conspicuous as refugees from central Europe, to have 'gone to ground.' It has been stated that Grunfeld, who was listed by the Island authorities as an alien but not as a Jew, was betrayed to the Germans by a fellow-worker. However that may be, it is inconceivable that the Germans, with their obsession for tracing racial origins, would have failed to establish her Jewish background, even without such malicious assistance.

Thérèse Steiner, Auguste Spitz and Marianne Grunfeld were arrested by the Germans almost two years after the invasion and were all three deported – or, from the German point of view, repatriated – to the Continent, probably via Saint-Malo, on 21 April 1942. This appears to have been part of a general round-up of foreign-born Jews living in France. The Guernsey deportees may have been held briefly at Rennes before being taken to Drancy concentration camp near Paris; it is now known that they were included in a group of 824 deportees transported by train from Drancy to Auschwitz on 20 July 1942. They are presumed to have been murdered on 23 July upon their arrival at Auschwitz – a mere 30 kilometres south-east of Grunfeld's birthplace at Katowice.

It is ironic that these three Jewish women should have escaped from their native Austria and Poland before the Nazi takeover and occupation of their respective homelands and found sanctuary in the British Isles, only to become stranded in the only British territory ever to be occupied by the Germans. There they suffered a double misfortune; to the British authorities – and of course national security in the Islands, especially in wartime, was a responsibility of the British Government – they were first and foremost under suspicion as aliens and two of them moreover were enemy aliens; by contrast to the Germans they were Jewish émigrés from territories which now formed part of Greater Germany who were ultimately to share the fate of Jews throughout Nazi-occupied Europe.

NOTE ON SOURCES

This article is based on a series of reports in the *Guernsey Evening Press* during 1991 and 1992, culminating in an account of a visit to Guernsey in January, 1993, by Professor Karl Steiner of Montreal, retracing the footsteps of his sister Thérèse. Perceptive articles by Major

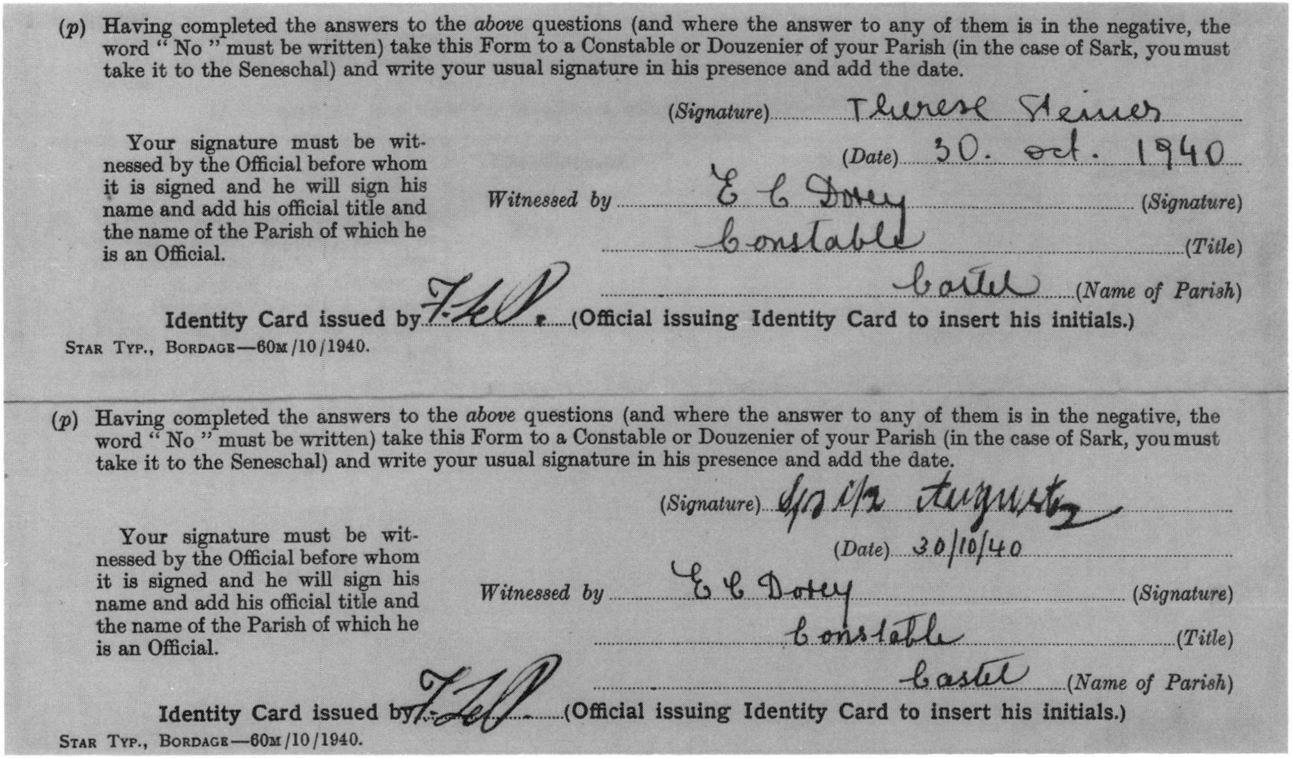

(*p*) Having completed the answers to the *above* questions (and where the answer to any of them is in the negative, the word " No " must be written) take this Form to a Constable or Douzenier of your Parish (in the case of Sark, you must take it to the Seneschal) and write your usual signature in his presence and add the date.

(*Signature*) Therese Steiner

(*Date*) 30. oct. 1940

Your signature must be witnessed by the Official before whom it is signed and he will sign his name and add his official title and the name of the Parish of which he is an Official.

Witnessed by E C Dorey (*Signature*)

Constable (*Title*)

Castel (*Name of Parish*)

Identity Card issued by F.L.P. **(Official issuing Identity Card to insert his initials.)**

Star Typ., Bordage—60m/10/1940.

(*p*) Having completed the answers to the *above* questions (and where the answer to any of them is in the negative, the word " No " must be written) take this Form to a Constable or Douzenier of your Parish (in the case of Sark, you must take it to the Seneschal) and write your usual signature in his presence and add the date.

(*Signature*) Spitz Augustey

(*Date*) 30/10/40

Your signature must be witnessed by the Official before whom it is signed and he will sign his name and add his official title and the name of the Parish of which he is an Official.

Witnessed by E C Dorey (*Signature*)

Constable (*Title*)

Castel (*Name of Parish*)

Identity Card issued by F.L.P. **(Official issuing Identity Card to insert his initials.)**

Star Typ., Bordage—60m/10/1940.

The signatures of Thérèse Steiner and "Auguste" Spitz on their respective registration forms. Although her name is typed as "Auguste", Miss Spitz appears to sign as "Augustey" – perhaps a variant of Augusta or Augustina? (The Greffe).

Edwin Parks on the question of the Jewish deportees appeared on 28 May, 1991 and 18 January, 1993. British government policy towards aliens generally is set out by Peter and Leni Gillman in *Collar the Lot - How Britain Interned and Expelled its Wartime Refugees* (Quartet Books Ltd, London 1980). They perhaps overstate the case against the authorities in London; in the summer of 1940 decisions had to be taken swiftly and on inadequate evidence. Internment for a year or two in the Isle of Man can hardly be compared with the fate of those who fell foul of the Nazi regime. The actions of the authorities in the Islands are discussed by Charles Cruickshank in the Official History (O.U.P., London 1975) and by Alan and Mary Wood in *Islands in Danger* (Evans Brothers Ltd., London 1955). As usual the Woods get to the heart of the matter in a few paragraphs – see page 67 – and the conclusions they arrived at still stand, despite the efforts of later writers in what is now a heavily tilled field. The Woods record, on page 67, their surprise that they could find no reliable details as to the ultimate fate of those Jews who were deported to the Continent, even from present members of the Jewish communities in the Islands. The reason is now clear; the women deported from Guernsey had no local connections; they were simply refugees from central Europe who had reached safety in Britain and had then suffered the tragic misfortune to be stranded in the Islands at the time of the German invasion.

JACK SAUVARY'S DIARY

J. C. Sauvary: "Diary of the German Occupation of Guernsey 1940-1945" edited by Miss K. A. Sauvary. The Self Publishing Association Ltd, Upton-upon-Severn, 1990. 313pp., illus., maps, glossary & index. £12.95.

In terms of content and presentation this is the best Occupation diary published to date. Miss Kitty Sauvary has produced a first-class edition of her father's diary; well illustrated, with an index, glossary of Island terms and place-names, brief notes on the principal characters, maps, menus and even a calendar of the Occupation years, the whole within a sturdy hard-back binding, this is a model of what self-publishing can achieve, and puts to shame many 'professional' publications. This detailed chronicle of daily life in occupied Guernsey by a well-informed observer is all the more valuable because death was to deny the writer the opportunity to revise his account prior to publication.

"Builder, Grower, Churchwarden, Douzenier": His business and social interests summarised thus on the title page, Sauvary was a recent widower aged 64 in June 1940 when the Occupation began. His children and grandchildren were all in England and it was for their information after the war that he started his diary, on 28th June, 1940, the day of the German air raid on the White Rock. The tone of the diary is conversational, as if, returning each day to his empty home, he was writing his impression of each day's events as an alternative to discussing them around the family hearth. He had, of course, to be cautious; in October 1940 he noted that "Many things I don't write about. It might not be prudent. I never know how things will turn out nor whose hands this epistle might get into."

Sauvary was a typical small Guernsey businessman of his era, combining horticulture, both outdoor and under glass, with general building and carpentry. He lived and worked near St Sampson's Harbour, which was in peace time the focus of the Island's granite export trade and was surrounded by quarries and stone-dressing yards. This industry, and commercial life in general, was dislocated by the evacuation to England of half the population prior to the German invasion.

Although immediately reduced, like almost every other civilian, to the humble bicycle as personal transport, Sauvary was in a better position than most to observe Islanders and occupiers alike. Severe shortage of motor transport, both personal and public, the curfew, German roadblocks and progressive malnutrition discouraged non-essential travel about the Island. Sauvary's carpentry business, and especially his activities as undertaker – a traditional carpenter's sideline – gave him occasion to travel. Funeral processions were forbidden from August 1941; mourners were limited to two carriages and they were not to follow the hearse; from February 1944 it was no longer possible to hire a motor hearse because of the petrol shortage. In addition his duties as churchwarden and douzenier (parish councillor) of St Sampson's kept him well-informed. In keeping with Island tradition, voluntary parish officers played an important role during the Occupation, when their local knowledge was valuable in, for example, the running of the Identity Card system.

If the evacuation in June 1940 left the Island half deserted, that gap was soon to be filled with a vengeance by German troops and their auxiliaries. At their peak in May 1943 there were 13,000 Wehrmacht personnel and 5,100 Organisation Todt workers in Guernsey. In a densely populated island occupiers and occupied lived cheek by jowl. There was no space for large scale manoeuvres and infantry and artillery exercises alike had to take account of the ever-present civilian population. On Saturday, 29th August, 1942, for example, Sauvary had occasion to cycle to Town; upon reaching the Royal Hotel, on the St Peter Port sea front, he saw "a German mock battle going on, soldiers posted at every pillar and corner. On my way back I got into the thick of it. I got off my bicycle and watched for a bit. Big guns and small tanks were firing, and rifle-shooting was going on." Soon however the battle ceased, familiar buildings emerged unscathed as the smokescreen cleared and the elderly Guernseyman cycled home to St Sampson's. The Germans were of course on invasion alert at this time, following the Dieppe raid on 19th August.

Schools, hotels and – to start with – empty houses, or their furniture, were commandeered wholesale as the garrison grew. On 18th May, 1942 Sauvary recorded seeing "a huge lorry going up the Vauquiedor with a lovely drawing-room suite, upholstered easy chairs, and 4 Germans sitting one in each. They looked so comfortable. They waved and laughed at me as they flew past." From October 1941 he himself had a succession of German officers and O.T. engineers billeted at his house; the following year he and many of his neighbours were evicted as the Germans set up a defended zone on the southern approach to St Sampson's Harbour. Soon afterwards Sauvary's carpentry workshop was demolished to make way for the extension of the O.T. railway network around the harbour.

Foreign labourers conscripted by the O.T. to build Fortress Guernsey were much in evidence as the St Sampson's quarries and timber yards were re-opened and work on the fortifications reached its peak in the summer months of 1942 and 1943. In November 1942 Sauvary noted that "just before daylight, at about 6.30, you hear the tramping of about 100 foreigners . . . I think they include every nationality. Many wear sacking over their head and tied with a cord around their neck, like a bonnet, and they work all day like that. One thing is certain, they will never stand our winter clad as they are. I am sure hundreds will die." He heard that on average 15 of the foreigners died each month.

Most accounts of the Occupation culminate in the joy and relief of Liberation in May 1945. For Sauvary however this was not to be. From early 1943 he had suffered increasingly from hoarseness and by August 1944 his voice had completely gone. Cancer of the throat was diagnosed but the expertise to treat it was not available in Guernsey; in December he was examined by a German surgeon at the military hospital at Le Vauquiedor (now the Princess Elizabeth Hospital) but with the same conclusion. Throughout the winter of 1944-1945 Sauvary hoped to secure travel to a neutral country for treatment under the auspices of the Red Cross, or for an early end to the war so that he might consult a specialist in London. These hopes were dashed, and he finally died at the Emergency Hospital on 5th April, 1945.

K.T.

CHANNEL ISLANDS OCCUPATION REVIEW – BACK NUMBERS

Readers wishing to complete their sets of the Review will be pleased to learn that a limited number of copies of past editions are still available for purchase, covering the years from 1973 onwards. Some are in very short supply while others are only available as photocopies. All the Reviews are well illustrated with maps and photographs. The principal features of recent Reviews are as follows:-

No. 16 (1988 Guernsey)	Alderney's German jetty, Evacuation of Guernsey school-children, German flamethrowers in Jersey (Pt.2), Loss of Speedball and Piccadilly Commando, German ground radar in the Channel Islands, La Mare sechsschartenturm, The story of the PT.509. 112pp. Original, £3.50
No. 17 (1989 Jersey)	Coastal artillery observation posts, Fortress covers into the occupied Channel Islands, The end of Resistance Nest Pavilion, Cézembre – a postscript, Operation Nest Egg – a narrative. 84pp. Original, £3.50.
No. 18 (1990 Guernsey)	The arrival of the occupying forces, Bundesarchiv Koblenz, Operation Green Arrow and the 216 Infantry Division in the Channel Islands, The 2cm Flak 30. 112pp. Original, £3.50
No. 19 (1991 Jersey)	Land mine warfare in the Channel Islands, The 319 Infantry Division in the Channel Islands, Disposal of Jersey's German coastal artillery weapons, Gun recovery – Stage one. 96pp. Original, £3.50.

The above prices include postage and packing. Payment should be in sterling by cheque drawn on a bank in the British Isles. Please send your order to the Guernsey Treasurer, Pierre Renier, at Le Plechon, Camp du Roi, St. Sampson's, Guernsey. We stock a wide range of Occupation publications and a full catalogue is available from the Treasurer.

COMMENTS AND CORRECTIONS

Errors and omissions can occur in the most carefully researched articles. The present Editor invites all readers to write in with details of any errors they may detect in, or with comments on, any item appearing in this or previous editions of the *Occupation Review*.

Occupation Review No. 18

Page 41: The sentry overlooks the glacis due east of the Citadel at Fort George; the buildings on the right are the married quarters above and to the west of the Lower Lines; neither Belvedere House nor the Fort Field are visible in this photograph, which appears to have been taken from the easternmost bastion of the Citadel.

Page 49: This machine gun position is at Icart Point (grid reference 318743 on the 1:21, 120 Ordnance Survey map of Guernsey supplied with the *Schedule of German Fortifications* drawn up by C.I.O.S. (Guernsey) and the view is westwards to La Moye Point, and not as captioned.

Herr Eberhard Schulze of Berlin, who served in the German army from 1938 onwards, and who was stationed in Guernsey for one year from the end of 1941, has written in describing *Occupation Review No. 18* as "most precise and objective". As an ex-regular soldier he draws attention to the following points of detail:–

Page 27: The figure on the right is not an officer but a sergeant (*Feldwebel*) as shown by the silver stripe on the epaulette and the N.C.O.'s silver stripe around the collar. Two further signs that he is not an officer are his boots and bayonet scabbard.

Page 34: The men are evidently forming up upon arrival at the airport. They are not a guard of honour, for which duty they would wear their steel helmets and remove their gas-mask containers.

Page 98: He confirms that *Uffz.* Oestmann violated at least two strict military rules, i.e. never to write where he is stationed and to destroy all letters received immediately. His handwriting, style of letter and mistakes suggest that he would have been about 35 years old and probably educated in a small town or in the country. "Active soldiers would have obeyed the rules." During the Ardennes offensive the Germans found letters from London girls to their American boyfriends from which it was possible to deduce where V1 rockets had landed, and to make corrections accordingly.

CAPTURED AT THE CASQUETS – AN ORNITHOLOGICAL FOOTNOTE

Ken Tough

The story of Operation Dryad, the British Commando raid on the Casquets lighthouse on 3rd September, 1942, is well known. The entire German crew of seven, who had failed to post a sentry, were surprised in the bedrooms and living rooms of the lighthouse, taken prisoner and removed to England. Less well known, however, is that the inglorious garrison had themselves effected a capture less than a week before.

Service on the Casquets rock was no doubt monotonous and unpopular, worse even than Alderney, which lay some eight miles to the east. The role of the crew was to keep visual and wireless watch, and to operate the light for brief periods to assist German shipping, as ordered from Cherbourg. Their current three month tour of duty had begun on 3rd August. For the first three weeks they saw neither ship nor aircraft; then on the afternoon of 28th August the tedium was relieved by the arrival of a carrier pigeon. Tired and hungry, the pigeon was snared and a green container was found attached to one leg.

It held a message written in French but only partially legible. The placenames Paris, Versailles, Granville, Boulogne and Dieppe could however be deciphered, and a reference to aircraft and hangers. It seemed that this was a message from the French resistance, destined for England, whose bearer had unwisely taken shelter on the Casquets rock in the face of a north-westerly gale. On 31st August the pigeon and the message were handed over to the Hafenkommandantur at Cherbourg.

The subsequent fate of the pigeon is not recorded.

SOURCE AND ACKNOWLEDGEMENT:

Full details of the interrogation of the prisoners taken at the Casquets are in the files of Combined Operations Headquarters at the Public Record Office, reference DEFE 2 109 ERD/4889. The writer is indebted to David Kreckeler for drawing this to his attention. The operation report on Dryad has been published in Winston G. Ramsey *The War in the Channel Islands – Then and Now,* (London, 1981), pp 141-145.